A Right Life:
Life Lessons for Young Christian Women

A Right Life: Life Lessons for Young
Christian Women

http://www.authorofmyfaith.com

Make it your goal to live a quiet life, minding your own business and working with your hands, just as we have instructed you before. Then people who are not Christians will respect the way you live, and you will not need to depend on others. -- 1 Thessalonians 4:11–12, NLT

How can a young person live a clean life?
By carefully reading the map of your Word.
I'm single-minded in pursuit of you; Don't let me miss the road signs you've posted.

I've banked your promises in the vault of
my heart So I won't sin myself bankrupt.
Be blessed, God; Train me in your ways of wise living.
I delight far more in what you tell me
about living than in gathering a pile of
riches. I ponder every morsel of
wisdom from you, I attentively watch how you've done it.
I relish everything you've told me of life, I won't forget a word of it. --
Psalm 19:9, MSG

I'm active duty Navy and towards the end of my tour in Okinawa, I participated in a Bible study called "College Group." Although I was beyond the age of the typical college student, I enjoyed the group because the participants truly did love God. They were studying the DVD series called the Truth Project. This DVD series really moved me and placed a seed for change in my life. The presenter talked about how God's Truth is often very different from man's truth in every area of life. I was in tears after the first session because the content made me realize there was so much more to life than what I was going through at the time. I realized that I had only scratched the surface of understanding the life God wants me to live.

But the young people in the group were the real blessing. In my interactions with them, I realized that these men and women had something I never had at their age—a real, live connection to, and relationship with, God. This is not because they were perfect or deeply rooted in God's word, but because they had a deeply rooted belief in His existence. They were open to inviting the Holy Spirit into their lives. And at that age, with so many distractions and demands, that's not an easy position to take.

These young people inspired me always to remember the person I was at their age, and to write this devotional so I could share what I wish I knew at that age. It's unfortunate that I learned these things on the other side of my youth, but all these Scriptures are powerful and life-changing no matter where you are in your faith and in which stage of life you may be. Ideally, though, these lessons are ones you want to embrace during early so that you can live a bold, right life for a long time. But with God, anything is possible. He makes each one of us beautiful in the right time—His time.

I truly believe that God led me to be a part of this group so that I could remember my youth without feeling shame. He doesn't want me to forget what that time of my life was like, but to learn from those experiences and share them with young Christian women. I've written these "life lessons" in the form of devotionals. I pray that each lesson will bless you so that you will come to know Him as the true and living God in your youth, learn how to "keep your way pure," and live a right life that screams the Truth very loudly.

Devotional Guide

THE RIGHT SELF-IMAGE: KNOWING WHO GOD IS, KNOWING WHO YOU ARE, AND KNOWING THE TRUTH ABOUT LIFE

I believe that in order to understand who you are, you have to understand who God is. Once I understood who He was, my life changed. My mentality and, consequently, my behavior changed. It was a process; I didn't arrive here overnight and I still don't always do what's right. But once you see God for who He really is, you can't go back to doing what you used to do and not feel convicted. You look at yourself differently and your purpose becomes crystal clear. Even when you make mistakes, you get back up and keep going because you know who God is and what He wants for you.

God is Always the Same

Jesus Christ (the Messiah) is [always] the same, yesterday, today, [yes] and forever (to the ages). -- Hebrews 13:8, AMP

This eternal sameness was a hard concept for me to grasp early in young adulthood because I thought that God's way of life was outdated. I didn't know that God's consistency throughout all ages was what made Him relevant to all ages. But if I knew then what I know now, I would have known early in my life what it meant to have a friend who sticks closer to me than a brother—no matter what or when. I also would have understood that this world in which we live is as much a product of man-made culture as it is the presence of God.

The culture of the days in which the Bible was written was drastically different than the life we live today, but not because God is different. People are different so the world is different. He left His Word to prove that He is the same—was, is, and will be. Bible commentaries and inspirational music may change to fit current culture, but God's message is the same.

We are told to live in this world and be a light in it. Therefore, you should use the culture around you to communicate the message of God; access people where they are. But, don't change God's message to fit into the culture around you. If you're up for the challenge, you've got a wonderful life ahead of you. With creativity, the sky is the limit when it comes to translating God's character and message into one that permeates and then changes current culture. With youth on your side, you have a lifetime to see the same message remain unchanged while evolving with the times.

Question for reflection:

How can God always be the same yet still be relevant throughout different generations?

God Can Get You "There"

For in Him we live and move and have our being; as even some of your [own] poets have said, For we are also His offspring. -- Acts 17: 28, AMP

When I was a teenager and a young adult, I did whatever I set my mind to. I definitely had my moments of indecision and doubt and my fair share in changes of heart. But, when I decided I was going to do something, I did it— good, bad, ugly or terrible. I truly did want to soar like an eagle, to live a good life, and achieve great goals.

What I missed at that age was that God could have gotten me there in much better fashion and form. I didn't know what I was created to do and I didn't understand that I was created to have my being in Him. I didn't know that flying only meant something when God was the one taking me there. But now I know that your youth is the time to soar to unimaginable heights, and that you can when you live and move and have your being in Him.

Question for reflection:

When in my life did I try to "get there" on my own?

God is Almighty, All-knowing and Indescribable

Many plans are in a man's mind, but it is the Lord's purpose for him that will stand. -- Proverbs 19:21, AMP

I've heard that the easiest way to get God to laugh is to tell Him your plans. But I know that as a young person it is easy to believe your plans are always rock solid and make perfect sense. One thing I have learned about God is that His ability to rule, plan and purpose is unimaginable. No matter how well I planned things out—or at least how well I thought I had—I would have done much better if I had submitted my plans to Him. I would have slept a lot better at night. I would have walked in my purpose much sooner in life. Through all my plans, I learned that God will have His way because now I'm doing the things He called me to do a long time ago, even though I ran from Him and went my own way. The next time you make plans, tell God you want Him to have His way with them and you. You'll be amazed at the results.

Questions for reflection:

What plans am I making now?

How should I submit those plans to God?

God is a Provider

The LORD is my shepherd; I have all that I need -- Psalms 23:1, NLT

As a young person, I know this may be hard to believe because it was hard for me to believe when I was in my twenties. There was always that newer and better car or electronic device or item of clothing out there. But looking back, I see how God gave me everything I needed. He never failed to address even the smallest detail of my life. I just couldn't see it because of the messages around me and because of my own limited thinking.

I know you grew up watching ads on TV for all kinds of video game systems, clothes, computers, toys . . . even food. And, this marketing has continued into your adulthood. So I understand why you might feel like you don't have what you need. That's the point of advertising — to get you to believe you need something that you really don't. Let's face it; we live in a capitalistic society where materialism and wealth are promoted. But despite what society says you don't have, God has already given you everything you need. You are not lacking anything. You don't have any need God can't meet. You are not incomplete. You are a work in progress and God is the author.

Question for reflection:

Why do I believe God hasn't already given me everything I need?

God Wants a Relationship with You

"For this is My Father's will and His purpose, that everyone who sees the Son and believes in and cleaves to and trusts in and relies on Him should have eternal life, and I will raise him up [from the dead] at the last day." -- John 6:40, AMP

It wasn't until I watched the Truth Project DVD series that I realized eternal life was about a relationship with God. Throughout my youth, I was taught that eternal life meant Heaven—or Hell. It was about the destination, not the personal connection. Once I started seeking God's face, I started to discover what God wanted from me and what the result of my obedience would be.

A relationship with Him is an experience that makes you more like Him, despite all your flaws, shortcomings, and human frailty. As the Scripture above states, He wants you to believe in Him, cleave to Him, trust Him, and rely on Him. To trust Him is to take Him at His word. This responsibility only can be accomplished if you take the time to read the Bible and meditate on what you read. Once you do this consistently, believing in Him, trusting Him, cleaving to Him and relying on Him becomes easier and easier. If you don't believe me, try Him. To trust someone you have to try them, give them a chance by placing your faith and very life in their hands. God will not let you down if you try Him.

Questions for reflection:

What would I have to change in my life right now truly to give God a try?

What are the benefits of eternal life with God?

You are *Young*…but GO FOR IT!

"Get the word out. Teach all these things. And don't let anyone put you down because you're young. Teach believers with your life: by word, by demeanor, by love, by faith, by integrity. Stay at your post reading Scripture, giving counsel, teaching. And that special gift of ministry you were given when the leaders of the church laid hands on you and prayed — keep that dusted off and in use." --1 Timothy 4:11-14, The Message

So what do you do when you're young, talented, eager to learn…and surrounded by older people who discount you because of your youth? Have you ever been told you don't know anything because you're too young and don't have any significant life experiences? You certainly could allow such negative and dismissive comments to deplete your energy. You could agree and believe you don't have anything to offer. Or, you could recognize that person for who he is — someone who resents your potential maybe because he squandered his own. Then, once you recognize this truth, go for it!

Don't let negative, resentful, bitter people steal your passion, your hunger or your drive. The sad truth is that any person older than you who proclaims you can't achieve your dreams because you're too young, is someone who has lost the capacity to learn and grow. When this happens, a person dies inside. So surround yourself with people who are alive emotionally and spiritually, who celebrate who you are and encourage your potential. If you can't find any such men or women right now, pray and ask God to show you how to encourage yourself until he brings people who can do this for you.

Don't listen to others who say you're "too young" to do what you're trying to do; if you believe them, soon you'll be telling yourself you're "too old" to do anything about it.

Questions for reflection:

On whom can I depend to celebrate my youth and the special gifts it offers?

How can I maintain a positive self-image in the face of people who discount me for my youth?

You Might Be Young *and* Inexperienced… but God Can Still Use You!

"And now, O LORD my God, thou hast made thy servant king instead of David my father: and I am but a little child: I know not how to go out or come in. And thy servant is in the midst of thy people which thou hast chosen, a great people, that cannot be numbered nor counted for multitude. Give therefore thy servant an understanding heart to judge thy people, that I may discern between good and bad: for who is able to judge this thy so great a people?" – 1 Kings 3:7-9, KJV

Solomon knew the deal. He knew he was young, inexperienced, and placed in a situation in which he was expected to perform beyond his ability. He was the heir to his father's throne but he had no idea how he was going to fill his father's large shoes. Still, he was confident that God would see him through.

When God appeared to him in a dream, Solomon only asked God for wisdom. But God was so pleased with the request, He made Solomon famous, fabulously rich, and the wisest king ever. Solomon ruled his kingdom with insight beyond his years because he had faith that God could use him even in his youth.

In reading this passage, it may look like Solomon actually doubted his own ability. But a closer look reveals that he knew God could do anything through him despite his lack of experience and knowledge. It was God, not Solomon, who would ensure that Solomon succeeded in his position.

Don't let your lack of professional experience, lack of knowledge or lack of life's inevitable testing keep you from going about the mission set before you. Ask God for wisdom above all else and watch Him use your youth in a powerful way.

Questions for reflection:

What am I facing right now that seems to be overwhelming considering my level of personal or professional experience?

How can I tap into God's wisdom and trust that He can help me be successful in my youth?

You are Strong in Your Youth

The glory of the young is their strength; the gray hair of experience is the splendor of the old. -Proverbs 20:29, NLT

God gave you vitality in your youth for a reason. Use it in a way so that when you are old and have a head full of gray hair, you can smile and laugh as you tell stories to your children and grandchildren about how God worked through you in your earlier years.

Ever wondered how fit you can be? Start conditioning your body now. Ever wondered just how far your talents could take you? Start nurturing them now. God uses people in every stage of their life—don't wait. You have strength now in order to discover the capacities of your body, mind, and spirit. Let your gray hair in old age represent a culmination of wonderful experiences in your youth—not missed opportunities and regret.

Question for reflection:

What can I do now to start discovering who I am?

You Can Recover

For a righteous man falls seven times and rises again, but the wicked are overthrown by calamity. -- Proverbs 24:16, AMP

You will make mistakes throughout your life. You're human; it's expected. Rest assured, though, that your youth is the best time to make bad choices and learn from them because this process is a part of discovering who you are. As this Scripture says, even the righteous fall many times. But they get back up.

Getting back up can be difficult. The embarrassment, the feeling that you've wasted your time and effort, the disappointment . . . it can feel like it's too much to bear. But just get back up and let your experience in falling make you wiser. God will be with you, even in your mistaken-prone youth, if you commit to Him—no matter how hard or how many times you fall. He delights in protecting and guiding you. So walk boldly knowing that He will help you get back up.

Questions for reflection:

What mistakes have I made from which I believed I would never recover?

How can I decide now to recover from mistakes I am sure to make in the future?

You are Not Called to Be Popular

It matters very little to me what you think of me, even less where I rank in popular opinion. I don't even rank myself. Comparisons in these matters are pointless. I'm not aware of anything that would disqualify me from being a good guide for you, but that doesn't mean much. The Master makes that judgment. -- 1 Corinthians 4: 3-4, The Message

Popularity is great for those who have it. But when you really think about it, popularity is based on the opinions and declared loyalty of other sinners. We are all sinners. We are broken and limited, which means that popularity is unstable at best. The acceptance you may feel now from peers is fleeting and rejection is inevitable at some point. But God will always see you with the eyes of love—even when you are at your worst. On the other hand, there are people in your life who will see your worst and end the relationship with you because your presence doesn't benefit them anymore. Not God. And that's why His judgment matters the most. No one else can come close.

Questions for reflection:

Why is popularity important to me?

What can I do to discover God's view of me and make that the only opinion that matters?

Life is Short and Full of Problems

How frail is humanity! How short is life, how full of trouble! – Job 14:1, NLT

If you live long enough, and this doesn't have to be many years at all, you will have problems. Sometimes you'll experience them in what seems like an unending series. If you don't know what that's like firsthand, read the book of Job. This man lost everything he had even though he was strong in his faith. Through that suffering, he realized how short and troublesome life really is. He also came to realize that God is in control of his life — even in the suffering.

Even though the story of Job is often used to teach us to accept God's will and persevere despite hardship and suffering, sometimes you need help moving on. If you are feeling stuck because of problems that are overwhelming you, seek help from a trusted counselor, pastor or friend. Life is too short to be stuck at any point because you don't know how to move forward. You don't want to live your whole life not knowing how to deal with the problems that come your way. Life is short and there is no guarantee that you will wake up the next morning or live another minute. Focus on what is important to Him and everything else will start to make sense. You'll gain a God-perspective on your problems.

Question for reflection:

How can I remind myself to focus on what truly matters?

Your Life has Meaning

All of us must die eventually. Our lives are like water spilled out on the ground, which cannot be gathered up again. But God does not just sweep life away; instead he devises ways to bring us back when we have been separated from him. -- 2 Samuel 14:14, NLT

The story of David is rich, colorful, triumphant, horrific and wonderful all at once. Before I studied this man, I used to wonder why someone who could mess up so badly could be blessed by God so greatly. I realized that it was because David got the point of life. No matter where he was or what he was doing, he feared, worshipped and was amazed by God. No matter how far he strayed from God, David eventually came back to the heart of who he was—a man who sought God's forgiveness, mercy, love and agenda. He knew that life without God was pointless.

At any moment your life can end. If it were to end today, what would it reflect? This isn't to make you feel as though you've fallen short in achievements or expected milestones. But the question is designed to make you think about where your relationship with God would be if you were to die today. If you need to go back to Him, He will accept you with open arms. He is always thinking of ways to draw you back to Him.

Questions for reflection:

Have I strayed from God in any area of my life?

If so, how can I go back to Him?

No Separation

And I am convinced that nothing can ever separate us from God's love. Neither death nor life, neither angels nor demons, neither our fears for today nor our worries about tomorrow — not even the powers of hell can separate us from God's love. No power in the sky above or in the earth below — indeed, nothing in all creation will ever be able to separate us from the love of God that is revealed in Christ Jesus our Lord. -- Romans 8: 38 – 39, NLT

God doesn't want anything to stand between Him and you. Unfortunately, as humans we are often trying to initiate this division through our own frailty. But, He still wants you to spend your life knowing His love and living in a way that demonstrates the knowledge that the two of you are inseparable. Life itself can get in the way, especially when you're young and you may not have experience in dealing with difficult events. God knows this and He wants you come to Him with all your concerns and worries. He wants you to tell Him when something bothers or scares you. He wants you to talk to Him when you've made what you believe is a horrendous mistake. You won't drive Him away. He loves you and He created a master plan that grants you direct access to Him. He doesn't want anything standing between you and Him. Not even you.

Questions for reflection:

Is there anything in my life that is standing between God and me?

How can I rearrange my life to keep us close?

God is Qualified

"...If God were not entirely fair, how would he be qualified to judge the world?" – Romans 3:6, NLT

God is fair and He is qualified to judge the world. In fact, He is the only one with the ability ultimately to determine what is right and what is wrong. There are so many different philosophies about life, its meaning and its purpose. The only one that is right is the one that is blueprinted in God's Word. His purpose is the reason we live. His way is the only right way. He himself gives meaning to life. If you want to know why you exist and what your purpose is, get into His Word. Once you do, you'll see that He truly is qualified — to judge, to rule, to love and to hold your life in His hands.

Consider this: God is fair and qualified to judge the world.

CONDUCT AND CONSEQUENCES

Early in my young adult years, I didn't fully understand the cause and effect relationship of conduct and consequences. Intellectually I did, but in terms of life experience — I didn't. The most important lesson I learned during that period is that you reap what you sow. More specifically, you reap *every* part of what you sow *every* day. Recognizing this fact builds habits, which forms your character, which forms the experiences you have in life. If you incorporate learning about God's Word into your life now as a young adult, knowing His will in difficult, trying and seemingly impossible situations will come easier than if you don't. God wants to be glorified in your conduct, and He's waiting to bless you when you constantly strive to be your best. Spend time in God's Word; what you sow will be magnificent.

Waiting

Even youths will become weak and tired, and young men will fall in exhaustion. But those who trust in the LORD will find new strength. They will soar high on wings like eagles. They will run and not grow weary. They will walk and not faint.-- Isaiah 40:30-31, NLT

Other translations of this Scripture use the word "wait" in place of "trust." I wish I knew earlier in life how to wait on God and trust Him to deliver His promises. But eventually I learned the difference between waiting on God, making things happen in my own strength or not even working for what I said I wanted. Whenever I tried to make things happen in my own strength I did not consult God. When I said I wanted something and didn't work for it, I knew what needed to be done but didn't do it. But I finally learned that when you are waiting on God, you are holding up your end of His promise to you by preparing to receive what He has in store for you.

You don't wish for your desire to happen and then literally sit and wait, though. You live your life in His strength and remember the promises He gave you. And the key to waiting on God is this: know what you're waiting on, know how to prepare for it, and then do just that. Your youth is an amazing time to let God place promises in your spirit and then prepare you for them. Even if you have to shift gears as God leads you, the preparation will not be in vain. Listening to God is always valuable.

Questions for reflection:

How do I need wait on God?

What can I start doing now to wait on God?

Sinning and Living a Life of Sin

My son, if sinners entice you, do not consent. -- Proverbs 1:10, NLT

Now remember I said we are all sinners. We have sinned, are sinning today, and will sin in the future. But I've come to learn that sinning and living a life of sin are two different things. Sinning is a temporary state because you repent, learn your lesson and move on. But living a life of sin eases you into a perpetual, blatant disregard for what you know is wrong. Perhaps such a distinction is what this parent was thinking when addressing his son in this verse.

Yes, we all sin, and God forgives us. But the best thing to do is to walk away from sin when it is presented to you, before you ever engage in the sinful behavior. It's easier said than done when you're just starting to make your way in life and you want to make and keep friends. But what true friend would urge you to do the wrong thing? What person who has your best interests at heart would encourage you to fall in your walk with God? To know which way to go and which way to avoid, you have to know what God's word says about sin. Don't be afraid of what He'll reveal to you. He loves you and only wants what's best for you.

Questions for reflection:

Have my friends ever encouraged me to sin?

What was my response?

Treasures vs. Death

Treasures of wickedness profit nothing, but righteousness (moral and spiritual rectitude in every area and relation) delivers from death. --
Proverbs 10:2

Understanding that "all that glitters isn't gold" was a lesson I had to learn the hard way as a young woman. Not because I was wicked, but because I often wanted things that others had without realizing what they had to do to get them. Think about it this way. You're struggling to make ends meet while doing things the right way and really trying to live a life pleasing to God. A friend, relative, associate or maybe even someone you don't know has something you have wanted for a long time. You no longer value doing the right thing because, for you, it doesn't provide the same results as more destructive approaches do for this other person. So maybe you adopt their tactics and schemes in order to get what they have. But what do you gain by doing that? Death. You might treasure something, but if you have to get it by evil means you will experience death in some area of your life—relational, spiritual, physical, or mental.

Doing things the right way may not get you what you think you treasure or get it to you in the time you want it…but at least you won't be in the clutches of death.

Questions for reflection:

What do I treasure?

Have I ever coveted something someone has? Why?

Preparation vs. Procrastination

He who gathers in summer is a wise son, but he who sleeps in harvest is a son who causes shame. -- Proverbs 10:5

I think this Scripture can be applied to several concepts, including hard work, diligence and timing. But I also think it can be applied to being prepared versus procrastinating. Chances are that if you gather during the summer, you'll probably reap the fruits of your work during the harvest. On the opposite end, if you slack off during the summer you won't reap a good or plentiful harvest in due season.

The summer in this Scripture refers to a time in your life when you need to be preparing for some goal, event or activity that takes place at a later date. The harvest represents that goal, event or activity. The more you prepare during the "summer" leading up to the "harvest," the more you will get out of your efforts. But the more you procrastinate, the more likely you will have poor or no returns on your input. It's easy to procrastinate. Sometimes you misjudge the amount of time and effort it will take to reach a goal; but sometimes, it's sheer laziness. Just remember that time you put into any endeavor will correlate to what you get out of it. Plan ahead and work hard to reap a bountiful harvest.

Questions for reflection:

Why do I procrastinate?

How can I break the habit?

Constructive Criticism is Necessary for Improvement

He who heeds instruction and correction is [not only himself] in the way of life [but also] is a way of life for others. And he who neglects
or
refuses reproof [not only himself] goes astray [but also] causes to err and is a path toward ruin for others. -- Proverbs 10: 17

Listening to constructive criticism is easier said than done. No one likes to have others point out their flaws, let alone be told how to correct them. But constructive criticism goes beyond the simple need to criticize and you need to know the distinction.

Criticism, jealousy, and mean-spirited behavior often come in the guise of constructive criticism from a person who envies you or needs to tear someone else down to make themselves feel or look good. However, true constructive criticism comes from people who have the genuine desire to share knowledge that will help you, whether they know you well or not, without any secondary motive. Ask God for a spirit of discernment to help you distinguish between these two types of messages. If you have a difficult time accepting and applying constructive criticism, start by finding a few good mentors you admire and can trust. Surrounding yourself with people who have been where you are, think highly of you and have your best interests at heart will help take the sting out of the criticism.

Questions for reflection:

(If I don't have any mentors) Who can I ask to mentor me and correct me?

(If I have identified mentors) What can I do today to build my relationship with my mentors?

How can I make sure I am open to constructive criticism?

God Will Know the Truth

For the Lord sees clearly what a man does, examining every path he takes. --Proverbs 5:21, NLT

You might tell yourself that your actions had good intentions. You might even fool others into believing the same thing. God, however, is never fooled. He knows you from the inside out and examines every part of you. It's one thing for you to examine your own motives. It's something completely different for God to examine them. If you're a caring, levelheaded and conscientious person, it's easy to see how something you plan to say or do will negatively affect someone else or even yourself. But no matter how much you review your intentions before you proceed, you always will view your actions with a blind spot. God sees all, knows all and understands all — and you don't. I don't. God is God and we are not. But if we welcome His examination of our hearts and lives and ask Him to reveal to us our own true motives, we can understand ourselves and others more clearly. All it requires is a willingness to be wrong, and to correct yourself when you are wrong. God will work with you on the rest.

Question for reflection:

Am I ready to learn my real motives for my behaviors? Why or why not?

Double Standards

False weights and unequal measures – the Lord detests double standards of every kind. --Proverbs 20:10, NLT

Double standards have always been a part of the way different groups are treated in society. As a young woman I always struggled with how it seemed to me that men in the Bible were allowed to be sexually immoral — be polygamists and treat women cruelly — yet women were stoned to death for acts such as adultery. Where was the man's culpability in this adulterous affair? At one point, this hypocrisy became a reason I didn't read or study the Bible like I should have. I couldn't reconcile in my mind how God's Word could promote love when it also had account after account of the subjugation and mistreatment of women.

I had to learn that sexual immorality, polygamy and sexism were never God's design and that manmade culture has a way of distorting His plan. It was man's twisting that was receiving all of my focus. I instead had to look at who God created me to be because His standard is the one that truly counts. So rather than be angry with the double standards of our culture and allowing it to distance you from God, keep learning His Word and seeking Him.

Also remember that God is always looking for people to use for His purpose in any era or culture. So let double standards be a starting point from which you learn more about God's laws. From there, you can liberate others trapped in the limitations of our culture.

Questions for reflection:

What double standards bother me?

What can I do to change them?

Never Argue with a Fool

Don't answer the foolish argument of fools, or you will become as foolish as they are. -- Proverbs 26: 4, NLT

It shouldn't be hard to ignore foolish arguments. Right? It really shouldn't. But in reality this is often more difficult than it seems. When wise people allow themselves to be sucked into the emotions and errors of foolish arguments, all their composure, wisdom and logic goes down the drain. The wise person becomes the fool.

So how do you avoid those who insist on provoking such silly arguments? State your case calmly and then walk away from the situation If their assertions include false accusations on your character or reputation, put your anger aside long enough to ask God how to deal wisely with the situation to keep it from elevating. God will always see things you can't see, so never forget to ask Him for His insight in dealing with people who stoop to foolishness.

Remember, the habits you develop in your youth are the ones that likely will create your character as an adult. If you make a habit of arguing with a fool, you'll argue with anyone. Then you might become the reason someone else starts crying out to God — asking for protection from your foolishness.

Questions for reflection:
What can make it so tempting to engage in foolish arguments?

What has been the outcome of such arguments in my life?

God Wants Your Mind

Don't copy the behavior and customs of this world, but let God transform you into a new person by changing the way you think. Then you will learn to know God's will for you, which is good and pleasing and perfect. -- Romans 12:2, NLT

What you think about your culture determines your relationship with God and, as a result, your growth as a believer. There are things that are acceptable and unacceptable in our culture—many of which are in direct opposition to what is revealed in God's Word. While I cannot always pinpoint who is creating these rules, I have noticed what seems to be acceptable in our culture as a whole. For instance, pre-marital sex is generally acceptable but, God's Word tells us clearly that any sexual act outside of the covenant of marriage is sin. If you stop to take a look at popular TV shows, books, magazines or other media and compare that to what you read in the Bible, you'll see some other glaring differences as well.

If you believe that you should conform to what our culture dictates when God's Word says such practices or behaviors are not permissible, you cannot become the person He wants you to be. On the other hand, if you are willing to be different and follow what God says is right and true, you can become who God wants you to be.

It does take time to become a new person. But the moment your mind changes, you cannot go back to doing what you used to do with a clear conscience. So then it's up to you to commit to align your actions and behaviors with what your mind is telling you is right.

Questions for reflection:

To which cultural customs do I conform?

What does God's Word say about these customs?

41

Look for God in Everything You Do

Trust God from the bottom of your heart; don't try to figure out everything on your own. Listen for God's voice in everything you do, everywhere you go; he's the one who will keep you on track. --
Proverbs 3:5-6, The Message

I'll be the first to tell you — trusting God is not always easy. I eventually learned, though, that it doesn't have to be a struggle. Trusting God can be a way of life in which you know what He's saying to you and you do it with no questions asked.

I didn't trust God for a long time. You also can't really trust someone you don't know, so I didn't know God for a long time. I didn't know Him because what I believed about Him was wrong. But one day, I came to see Him for who He really was. He spoke to me clearly through a scripture that let me know that He was and always will be the only one I can really trust. Since then I haven't been the same. I trust Him with my life and I'm unhappy when I'm not seeking Him. I'm unhappy when I'm walking out of His will. I'm unhappy when I allow my circumstances to make me doubt His promises and His love. I'm heartbroken when — because of my own mistakes and pain — I can't hear from Him. I don't want to figure my life out on my own because I already know how that turns out. I want to acknowledge Him at every turn and invite Him into my life — even if I can't feel Him. He is everywhere and He wants to show you which way to go. If you trust Him, you will never go wrong.

Questions for reflection:

Has trusting God been difficult? Why or why not?

Why should I trust God?

Don't Assume That You Know It All

Don't be impressed with your own wisdom. Instead, fear the LORD and turn away from evil. -- Proverbs 3: 7

I don't know anything compared to what God knows about me, this world and everyone and everything in it. I do know, though, that hearing from God and doing what He says is much better in any situation than just doing whatever seems wise or right to me. Even though He gives you the choice to obey Him or go your own way, His way is the only way that is right.

It is true that God can give you wisdom, and you should seek that. But the minute you gauge your life using your own wisdom and without including God, you are susceptible to taking a wrong turn. Many choices and behaviors might seem wise in your own eyes at any given moment. But if you act without God's wisdom, even the best of intentions can become evil.

Relying on your own wisdom can lead to pride. When you become proud of your own abilities, you tend to forget that God was the one who gave them to you in the first place. When you become proud of your own wisdom, you forget that God is the source of that wisdom. But when you respect God and constantly remember His generosity towards you, you focus on His purpose for your abilities rather than your own. Don't fall into the trap of believing your own wisdom is sufficient. Give God His due and thank Him for what He's done.

Questions for reflection:

How can I avoid the trap of believing that my own wisdom is sufficient?

How can I rely on God's wisdom in all areas of my life?

Discipline is Love

My child, don't reject the LORD's discipline, and don't be upset when he corrects you. For the LORD corrects those he loves, just as a father corrects a child in whom he delights. -- Proverbs 3:11-12

Receiving God's discipline was an easy concept for me to grasp until I was personally on the receiving end of His correction. Discipline hurts; it hurts your feelings, your ego, and your pride. Sometimes discipline can be embarrassing when it involves other people who have to correct us in light of our poor choices or our behavior. Discipline also can shatter your sense of reality if you truly believed that your way was the best way to handle the situation you were facing.

The good news is that God corrects us because He loves us. He doesn't want us to go through life struggling with issues, behaviors, attitudes and deficiencies that keep us from His best, especially when we can change them. He wants to see us constantly striving for our full potential. In order to do that, He has to correct us because none of us is perfect. We all have weak areas and He knows every detail of them. If you can get past your selfish feelings about being corrected, you'll see that it can save your life.

Questions for reflection:

What areas of my life might God be trying to discipline?

How can I lower my defenses to receive His discipline?

Believing God Despite What the World Says

God is not man, that he should lie, or a son of man, that he should change his mind. Has he said, and will he not do it? Or has he spoken, and will he not fulfill it? -- Numbers 23:19

You are at a stage in your life when you are expected to figure out what career path you will take, what type of woman you want to be, and where you will go in life. Some of you have been encouraged to live out your dreams. Others have been told to get your heads out of the clouds and make these decisions with a practical and logical approach. But if God gave you a talent, a passion, a vision or a dream in your youth, He will show you how to fulfill it. Will you listen to parents, family and friends who tell you to take the route that society says we should take? Or will you listen to the God who made you, gave you your being and talents, and will see you through?

I'm sure that your friends, family and loved ones really do want what's best for you and want you to succeed. But ultimately, they cannot tell you what you were created to do — only God can. God cannot lie. If He told you something will come to pass in your life, you will experience it if you do what He is calling you. If you don't, you'll eventually see consequences for not following the vision He gave you.

Questions for reflection:

Has God planted dreams, visions and goals in my heart? If so, what are they?

Is what God has planted different from the path my friends, family and loved ones are expecting me to take? If so, what should I do?

Choose to Live Life on God's Terms

I am the vine; you are the branches. If you remain in me and I in you, you will bear much fruit; apart from me you can do nothing. – John 15: 5, NLT

You can do whatever you want because God gave you free will and the ability to choose which way to go. But God wants you to choose His way. This Scripture says that you cannot do anything apart from Him. What does this mean?

God wants you to choose the life He can give you. He knows you are young and have this energy and desire to forge your way in life. And He knows He gave you the capacity to choose your own path. But what He has for you will give you true and everlasting life. And it will always be more than anything you can do apart from him. Remain in Him. Read His word. Get to know Him. Know His voice. Then you'll know His fruit when you see it grow in your life.

Questions for reflection:

How can I remain in God?

Are there some examples in my life of the fruit that God has already allowed to grow?

Focusing on God

Give careful thought to the paths for your feet and be steadfast in all your ways. Do not turn to the right or the left; keep your foot from evil. -- Proverbs 4:26-27, ESV

So now you know that God wants you to choose life abiding in Him. But what about the successful people you admire who clearly have not chosen God's way? Surely you see peers and older adults living the good life, succeeding in every area of their lives . . . and they aren't even Christians! Or maybe they are, but you can't tell.

Well, you don't have to believe in God to become successful by worldly standards. You don't have to believe in God to be a kind, wealthy, or good person. But the truth is that God created this world and He created the paths for all of us to take. What God has for you is for you alone. Don't look to the left or right. If you become consumed with the fruits of those who don't believe in or follow God, you eventually will compromise your own relationship with Him for fruit that does not represent or glorify Him. As a result, you'll miss out on what He has for you.

If you want success in your life, focus on how to cultivate the fruit of a relationship with God in your life. Then people who don't believe in God or have turned away from Him will wonder how to get what YOU have.

Questions for reflection:

Why is it easy to get distracted by what others are doing?

How can I focus only on what God has for me?

Trying to Trick God

Don't be misled: No one makes a fool of God. What a person plants, he will harvest. -- Galatians 6:7, MSG

A common belief held by young women is that they are invincible. You see tragic news stories or hear about a friend's misfortune and think, "That would never happen to me." But it can . . . especially if you're engaging in the same behaviors that led to these results. You may ask, "But what about the people who sin grossly and never pay the price?" God sees everything. He may not correct that person in the way or in the timeline you feel He should. But what you put into your life is what you will get back. What you give will be returned to you.

If you start now living a life that is pleasing to Him, you will not regret it. If you're not sure how to do that, just ask Him to guide you and He will. But remember that you are not invincible. There are consequences to your choices, both now and later. God sees you clearly and is always waiting for you to choose His way.

Questions for reflection:

What times in my life (if any) did I believe I was invincible?

What was the result?

Trust God's Timeline

He has made everything beautiful in its time.... -- Ephesians 3:11, AMP

I had to break this verse down into three days and in three days you'll see why.

My mother's Godmother gave me a high school graduation card that included this verse. I was not in a place in my life where I could fully appreciate the beauty of this verse. Yet somehow I knew this verse was telling me that one day my life would start.

Think about a flower. When have you ever seen a flower bloom before its time? It needs sun, rain and healthy soil to blossom. It might seem like the rain will never end. The sun might be so hot you feel like you're in a desert with no oasis in sight. The soil might make you feel like you're surrounded by complete darkness and silence. Just know that these elements are all necessary for your life to blossom in God's own time.

Trust God's Purpose

. . . He also has planted eternity in men's hearts and minds [a divinely implanted sense of a purpose working through the ages which nothing under the sun but God alone can satisfy]... --
Ephesians 3:11, AMP

I cannot wrap my mind around the concept of eternity from God's perspective. I only understand that it is forever and that our lives on earth are a small portion of that forever. But since God invented time, He *can* see what we can't from beginning to end - whatever that eventual end may mean in terms of forever.

The second part of this verse lets me know that I can understand what my divine purpose here on life is because God planted a part of eternity within me. He planted it in us all. And it is the part of eternity he chose to share with us. This part of the verse also says nothing else can satisfy this sense of purpose. It's never too early to ask God why he put you here. You're never too young to fulfill your purpose. Use your youth to discover it so that while you're still young you can help new generations do the same.

Trust God's Lack of Revealed Details

...yet so that men cannot find out what God has done from the beginning to the end. -- Ephesians 3:11, AMP

God plants the sense of purpose, but He doesn't reveal His main plan to us. This might seem like He's leaving you in the dark. But in reality, God is God and we are who we are. God is all-knowing, all-powerful and he is everywhere. We are His creation but we are limited beings and cannot fully comprehend His works. We are all made differently so that we can complete His ultimate plan. We do not need to know the entire design, just our role in it.

Embrace what makes you unique because no two people are alike. If you don't know what makes you unique, ask God to show you. The sooner you embrace what makes you unique, the more time you have to "perfect" it!

GUIDANCE, MENTORSHIP AND COUNSEL

To have a mentor as a young adult is one of life's best kept secrets. Honest people who truly care about you and the purpose God has for your life and who are willing to share information that will make your life better — this is priceless. If you're willing to heed their guidance, you can avoid the same mistakes they made and make faster strides in your spiritual progress.

The Right Answer

We can make our own plans, but the Lord gives the right answer. --
Proverbs 16:1, NLT

As a young Naval officer — young in age and young in experience — I had to rely on a lot of assistance in learning my job. Sometimes I would spend hours going through an instruction manual trying to find an answer to a problem. However, when I determined to ask someone higher in rank for advice and guidance, I often received an answer in only minutes. These older officers had several years of experience in doing what I was recently appointed to manage.

God specializes in providing answers and solutions to all situations, and offers those based on where we are in life. You grow wise in experience as we age (usually), so it is natural to conclude that you will become better equipped to plan your life as you get older. God likes young go-getters. But He loves young go-getters who ask Him for the right answer and who are willing to humble themselves to His direction. He wants you to have the desires of your heart, but He wants you to choose His way. Make your plans. Just don't forget to ask God to give you the final and right answer.

Questions for Reflection:
Have I ever taken action based only on what I planned? What were the results?

How could those times have turned out differently if I had asked God for the right answer before I took action?

When the Right Way Leads to Death

There is a way which seems right to a man and appears straight before him, but at the end of it is the way of death. -- Proverbs 14:12, NLT

I believe this Scripture is telling us that none of us has the ability independently to judge what is good and what is evil. When we commit to reading the Bible and learning to follow God, we can gain an understanding of what is right and wrong because the Bible is truth. But without God and His Word, the definition of right and wrong varies depending on who you ask. I know from experience that anytime we take a path or engage in a behavior that we believe is right without consulting God's Word and without listening to the Holy Spirit, we run the risk of death.

Sometimes we really do make choices believing that what we're doing is pleasing to God. But when it becomes evident that we made the wrong choice, we need to go back to God's Word. People might tell you that you're young, that you have the rest of your life ahead of you, and that now is the time to do what young women do and make mistakes. This is not godly counsel. Yes, your youth is meant for exploration and discovery—but within the boundaries that God designed. If you don't know what those boundaries are, pray and ask God to help you learn and ask a godly friend or trustworthy spiritual leader. God wants you to use your youth to discover wonderful things about yourself, not make poor choices that lead to death.

Consider this: God wants you to enjoy your life and is not withholding opportunities for joy. If He doesn't allow something to happen in your life it could be for your own good. If He is convicting you to change, it's because He loves you and wants to put you on the right path.

Learning from the Lives of Others

The teaching of the wise is a fountain of life, that one may avoid the snares of death. -- Proverbs 13: 14, AMP

Godly mentors are those who manage every area of their lives by the instructions given in God's Word. They are influential because God has given them wisdom that other people seek. They are generous with what they have and therefore are rightfully in a position to help someone else — financially, spiritually or practically. They are approachable, will not repeat what you discuss and will be open and honest with you about your strengths, weaknesses and mistakes. They also will share relevant information about themselves to help you learn.

I didn't have a godly mentor until later in my young adulthood and I know I would have been truly blessed if I had such a person earlier in life. Although God blessed me in other ways, it wasn't until I met my mentor that my faith ramped up to a new level and I started taking action on the things that He put in my spirit years ago. And because this person poured into my soul, I experienced the fountain of life that is the focus of this scripture. I learned from my mistakes and, because I grew spiritually, I started to avoid the same traps to which I found myself susceptible when I was younger. Ask God to give you a godly mentor in your youth, and you'll experience a fountain of life, too.

Consider this: No one knows everything, and sometimes you need others to point out your weaknesses and blind spots. Always look for godly mentors who can give you godly counsel.

When Advice Counts

Plans succeed through good counsel: don't go to war without wise advice --Proverbs 20:18 NLT

I find it interesting that this Scripture advises us not to go to war without wise counsel. It seems like a given, but military war is not the only war in life. There is a war for our souls, minds, bodies and lives. Satan wants to destroy us, but God wants to use us to fulfill His purposes.

Every day is a battle for your spirit, so it would deeply benefit you to understand how to win the war. You do this by learning the Word of God and by asking Him to teach you how to live and how to win this war. Sometimes He wants you on the front line. Sometimes He wants you hidden. Sometimes He wants you in the watch tower. Sometimes He wants you to help deliver others from the enemy's traps. Sometimes He doesn't want you waging war at all. But you can't really know this unless you seek His wise advice and counsel. Get in the habit of asking God what the game plan is every day before your day starts and you can't go wrong. Know what the plan is before you go to war.

Consider this: God always will give you wise counsel if you know His voice. He also uses people in your life to speak wisdom and provide godly counsel. Learn how to recognize these types of people and be open to their counsel.

WORK, WORK ETHIC, AND FINANCES

I wish I had known early in my adulthood that God was lord over my professional life and my finances. Instead, I believed that I was left on my own to manage these areas of my life. If I knew then what I know now, God truly would have used me to glorify Him in these areas. I realize now that I had tremendous opportunities to be a witness to God's goodness just through my professional life alone. I missed them because I was not rooted in the Word of God and because I didn't nurture my relationship with Him. Don't miss out. You're not too young to honor God with your work and finances.

Diligence Will Make You a Ruler

The hand of the diligent will rule, but the slothful will be put to forced labor. -- Proverbs 12:24

This Scripture doesn't say that the rich, wise, intelligent or most capable will rule. It says that those who are diligent will rule. To be diligent you have to be consistent, regardless of your circumstances and how they may change. Circumstances often dictate and influence how we feel, and how we feel often dictates how much we get done. If you can learn how to push past how you feel and stay on track, you can do what God is calling you to achieve.

To achieve your goals despite how you feel does not require you to deny how you feel. Instead, acknowledge how you feel, take time to deal with it, re-focus on the goal, and then take the steps you need to take to get there. Have a clear goal and know why you have the goal — which is easy when you ask God what the goal should be. When you have the goal, focus on it despite your emotions and don't change the goal to suit your emotions. Cry if you have to, but work while you're crying. Whatever you do, learn how not to give up on your goal. If you do this enough times as a young person, it becomes a wonderful habit to have later on in life.

Questions for reflection:

In which areas of my life am I diligent?

What can I do to stay diligent in these areas and also become diligent in others?

A Career You Love

The blessing of the Lord – it makes [truly] rich, and He adds no sorrow with it [neither does toiling increase it]. -- Proverbs 10:22, AMP

This world would be an amazing place if everyone had a job that they loved. Hating your job or career field is one of the saddest things in life because most of us spend at least eight hours of every day for five days every week at our jobs. In one week that is forty hours and in just one year that's 2,080 hours. That's a lot of hours to spend disgruntled, miserable and wishing you were somewhere else. Now, I'm not saying you shouldn't be grateful for a starting point or that you shouldn't be thankful to have a job. I'm also not telling you to quit a job just because you hate it. But what I am saying is that if you hate your job to the point that you feel sick whenever you have to go or dread waking up in the morning, maybe these are signs that you need to start thinking about where God may want you to go, whether it means changing jobs or changing yourself to stay on the job.

I believe God wants you to be grateful for the blessings He gives you. But I also believe that some blessings are only temporary, and that dissatisfaction can be His way of reminding you that you need to step into or take a step closer to what He put you on this earth to do. Now is the best time to figure out what your calling is and to nurture your talents. Once you do, focus on how to use them to have meaningful, fulfilling work in your life.

Questions for reflection:

Am I fulfilled by my current job? Why or why not?

What can I do to have a career I love?

Have a Goal, Then Do What It Takes to Reach It

He becomes poor who works with a slack and idle hand, but the hand of the diligent makes rich. -- Proverbs 10:4

I like this verse because it challenged me to think about Proverbs 12:24, referenced in an earlier devotion, from the perspective of devising an action plan. It gives a better understanding of what both laziness and hard work look like. Laziness is a slack and/or idle hand. Slack means you don't do your best while idle means you do too little or nothing at all. Overall, the task at hand is not a priority and so it's treated like a project that can be shelved at any time.

The opposite of lazy is hard-working. This means that no matter the circumstances, or how you feel, you make the time to complete the task at hand to achieve the ultimate goal. You know what the goal is and why it's the goal. You do not give up until you achieve it or God tells you to give it up. Laziness works under the right conditions. Hardworking is committed regardless of the conditions. So you have to decide. Do you want to develop the skills now in your youth that will help make you "rich"? Or are you going to focus only on what you want now and be "poor" later on in life?

Questions for reflection:

What are my short-term goals? What are my long-term goals?

How will I achieve them?

Live Within Your Means

The wise have wealth and luxury, but fools spend whatever they get. -
- Proverbs 20:20

Sometimes wealth is acquired by saving and spending wisely. If you don't believe me, take a look at how many Americans drive Hondas but park them in the garages of homes that cost hundreds of thousands or a few million dollars. Likewise, look at how many Americans drive a luxury car but park them in the parking lots of their apartment complexes. We all make choices concerning financial priorities. It's not wrong to have nice things or live a life of luxury. It is problematic, though, when you spend everything you make and then even spend more than you make. Living in luxury with no savings only proves you think in terms of what you want now or what you're told you should have right now. If you learn early how to manage your finances and discipline yourself in your spending, you'll be more like the wise who live in luxury.

Questions for reflection:

Why do I believe that living in luxury is desirable?

How can I work toward having savings while spending within my means?

Know Where You Excel and Master It

Do you see a man diligent and skillful in his business? He will stand before kings; he will not stand before obscure men. -- Proverbs 22: 29

I view this Scripture on two levels. First, the person who is skilled in a craft or ability and diligently uses and improves it will be known by those in power, authority or leadership — the decision-makers. Second, decision-makers only want the best on their team.

As a young adult, you have the advantage of time to hone and strengthen your abilities. If you become the best you can be, you won't have to worry about competition because there will be no one who can complete a task like you do. You never can completely master a skill or subject of knowledge because there is always more to learn that will take you to the next level. But as long as you master your craft at each level, until the next learning opportunity comes along, you're doing exactly what God wants you to do. Take this time in your youth to develop your craft, your confidence and your leadership potential. You never know where God will take you or who He'll put in your path – so be ready.

Questions for reflection:

What abilities and talents do I have? How can I improve them?

How can I use them for the benefit of others in God's earthly kingdom?

What Laziness Will Get You

Laziness leads to a sagging roof; idleness leads to a leaky house. --
Ecclesiastes 10: 18, NLT

At first I found it interesting that this Scripture does not say that poverty leads to a sagging roof and a leaky house; this takes both laziness and idleness. But it makes sense. Some of the most industrious, brilliant and hard-working people are working class or were at one time. While they may not be rich or have the finest things in life, they are good stewards over what does belong to them.

The Bible says that to whom much is given, much is required. But often, people who receive much without having to work for it don't value hard work or understand the importance of a strong work ethic. You can never go wrong with hard work and its resulting productivity. If you find it difficult to give your all to your current job or life situation, it could be time to consider shifting gears and asking God if it's time for you to move on. Or, maybe you just need to reconsider your attitude towards your responsibilities in life. Either way, God wants to bless you with a life that results from hard work and productivity.

Questions for reflection:

Am I giving my all to my current job or life situation?

Why or why not?

Perfect Conditions

Farmers who wait for perfect weather never plant. If they watch every cloud, they never harvest. -- Ecclesiastes 11: 4, NLT

When you use imperfect conditions as an excuse to avoid doing something, it's time to be honest about the real reason you don't want to do it. Many tasks are tedious, annoying, and maybe even boring, but they are necessary to achieve an ultimate goal. More importantly, God is watching how you respond to adversity and difficult circumstances. He wants to know that He can trust you to persevere in spite of your circumstances. When He sees you consistently working and giving your all even during those undesirable moments and knows that you're doing it to please Him, He will reward or promote you in the right time.

Your circumstances are not the driving factor in how much you can actually attain. Your determination, your faithfulness, your belief in God and His power, and your willingness to see a thing through will get you where you wish to be — provided that it's what He wants for you.

If you can learn to be happy when you don't have everything you want, you will be happy when you do. If you always have to have the ideal conditions in which to operate, you soon will find that you never are happy. Chances are that what you desire will not come with perfect conditions. God wants to bless you, but He wants to know that you can be happy with the blessing. A young person who is happy and productive regardless of what life brings is an awesome example of what God can do.

Questions for reflection:

Are there conditions in my life that are undesirable?

How can I be happy and productive despite these conditions?

Investments

But divide your investments among many places, for you do not know what risks might lie ahead. -- Ecclesiastes 11: 2, NLT

The saying "never put all your eggs in one basket" may sound cliché, but it's true. What it means is that you should establish multiple streams of income, invest wisely in savings and retirement plans, and never put all your confidence solely in the job market or your ability to work for a long period of time. It is wise to consider various opportunities for wealth and prosperity, especially when you're young. You won't be this age forever, and there is no guarantee that you'll be healthy enough to work the time that's required for retirement with a company. There's also no guarantee of job security in any job market. While some markets are more stable than others, the truth is that any company can go under at any given moment. But when you ask God to help you understand where to invest your time, finances, talent, and professional energy, the sky is the limit.

Today, stop and think about what it would take to ensure financial stability in the later and final stages of your life. Now is the best time to do this since time is likely still on your side.

Questions for reflection:

What does God's Word say about acquiring wealth and financial stability?

How can I apply these principles to my life now?

When God is Your Boss

Work with enthusiasm, as though you were working for the Lord rather than people. -- Ephesians 6:7, NLT

At some point in your life, whether you love or hate your job, you will have a crazy boss. Or maybe you will be the crazy boss because you manage or lead people who would drive anybody crazy. Or, perhaps you may find yourself with growing dissatisfaction, reducing your output to the bare minimum required to get the job done. You also might face situations that cause you to lose the faith or confidence you once had in the company for which you work.

This verse makes it clear what your response to an unhappy work situation should be. You are to work as if God is your boss. That changes things, right? I hope so. Because when God is your boss and you strive to be the type of employee He would want you to be, you become an asset to any company. Unfair treatment, unbearable conditions, and difficult personalities are no longer factors that keep you struggling in your position. They instead become the tools God uses to mold you into His type of employee. If you really want to learn what type of boss God is and what type of employee He wants you to be, read His Word and ask Him how you can improve. Just be ready to take on the challenges He gives you and the changes He makes evident to you.

Questions for reflection:

What type of employee would God think I am right now?

What does God's Word say in regards to the type of employee I should be?

DEPRESSION, ANXIETY, FEAR, ANGER, BITTERNESS

Mental illness and distress are the manifestation of chemical or physical imbalances, wrong thinking and spiritual attacks on the mind. Young women are not immune. In fact, I believe that you may be even more susceptible to it at times because you are still learning who you are. But God's Word offers comfort and guidance on this issue. And if you need help, never be ashamed to ask and receive it. God wants you whole, healthy and able to live out the abundant life He has for you.

Anxiety

Don't worry about anything; instead, pray about everything. Tell God what you need, and thank him for all he has done. Then you will experience God's peace, which exceeds anything we can understand. His peace will guard your hearts and minds as you live in Christ Jesus. -- Philippians 4:6-7, NLT

It is so easy for someone else to tell you not to be worried or anxious, and that being worried means you have no faith in God. There are so many causes for anxiety; others may not understand why you are experiencing stress when the same set of circumstances might cause them no worry whatsoever. Please remember — facing a life situation you're not prepared for or able to deal with does not always mean that you lack faith in God. But if you hold on to God an don't give up, He will strengthen you and show His power in your life through these difficult situations.

Consider that the spiritual implication of anxiety is that you are trying to do something in your own strength. That just means that you don't have enough trust in God to help you deal with whatever you're facing. God never intended for you to deal with anything — distress, turmoil or trauma — in your own strength. He wants you to trust Him and continually ask Him to guide you during these times. But please know that while He is the ultimate help and covering, sometimes you do need to seek professional help from competent mental health care providers. Medication under their care also can help get you back on the right track. Ultimately, you have to talk to God and seek His will for restoration because He's really the one who can reach you where you are and give you what you need to get past your anxieties. He will hear you and give you peace. He also can use others to help you overcome when you're ready for help.

Questions for reflection:

What am I struggling with now that seems overwhelming?

What resources are available to help me overcome this problem?

When God Seems Far Away

O Lord, why do you stand so far away? Why do you hide when I am in trouble? -- Psalm 10:1, NLT

David had many reasons to be distressed. He was a military officer during wartime. His predecessor tried to kill him on several occasions by pinning him to the wall with a spear. His very best friend was killed in a battle. The people on whom he had to rely had no loyalty to him whatsoever. He had more enemies than allies. And on top of everything, even though he really did love God, he made several poor decisions that resulted in people getting hurt and losing their lives. I could see why he felt like God was far away. I could see why he resorted to hiding and sin. He had no peace.

Distress can be one of the many signs of sin. When you sin, distress usually manifests itself in your life through negative emotions like anger, depression and fear. But sometimes sin is the result of not being able to cope effectively with the life situations that you did not choose and over which you have no control. Either way, sin distances you from God. So the issue is not that God has abandoned you, but that sin has put distance between you.

Don't stay focused on who is to blame for the sin. Focus on what you need to do to make it right between you and God, then repent. If you can't find your way back on your own, ask for help from someone who you know is qualified to assist you. He doesn't want to be far away from you. He wants to be close and help you deal with whatever is troubling you.

Questions for reflection:

What sins do I have in my life?

How can I close the distance between God and me?

Look to God for Help

The Lord is a shelter for the oppressed, a refuge in times of trouble. --
Psalm 9:9, NLT

I remember the first time I heard this Scripture. Although I didn't consider myself as being oppressed, I did see that I felt powerless. Because I didn't know who God really was, I kept looking to those He had appointed in authority positions in my life to do what only He could do. It took disappointment after disappointment to get me to the point where I finally just threw my hands up to God and cried out, "What do you want from me?" At that moment, I became fertile soil for God to show me who He really was, and since then I haven't been the same.

What this Scripture is saying is that God is the one in whom you should have absolute trust and confidence because He's the one who will protect you. He wants you to run to Him when you are in trouble. He's the only safe haven in this world. This also means that God will never call you to do something for someone else that only He can do for them. God wants the place in our lives that only He can have. Let God show you how to make Him your refuge now and for the rest of your life.

Questions for reflection:

Who do I turn to when I'm afraid and I need help, and why?

Who should I turn to when I'm afraid and I need help, and why?

Only Fear God

The fear of man brings a snare, but whoever leans on, trusts in, and puts his confidence in the Lord is safe and set on high. -- Proverbs 29: 25, AMP

Being afraid of people will cost you a close relationship with God. It's easy to say that you fear God and not other people until you realize those other people are your boss, your friends, your family members, or people who have access to resources you need. But the first part of this verse couldn't be any clearer. Fearing others is a trap. Yes, other people can do terrible things to you, but God is the only one who can truly keep you safe.

You also have to understand that your idea of safety may not be God's definition of safety. You can literally always be in danger — whether of your design or not — and still be safe. In fact, you actually must have threats in order for God to keep you safe. That's where dependence, trust and confidence come into play. You can become confident in God's ability to keep you just by reading the Bible. You come to trust Him by watching Him use dangerous situations and circumstances in your life for good. You come to depend on Him when you've experienced enough to believe you can't do it alone. Take it from someone who knows . . . trust Him, depend on Him and put your confidence in Him. Don't fall into the trap of fearing man.

Questions for reflection:

Who do I fear? Why?

Do I fear God as much as or more than I fear them? Why or why not?

Know Where You Can Go When You're in Trouble

The name of the Lord is a strong tower; the [consistently] righteous man [upright and in right standing with God] runs into it and is safe, high [above evil] and strong. -- Proverbs 18: 10

The *consistently* righteous person runs to God and is protected and safe. I know what you may be thinking because this statement once made me feel condemned, too; I wasn't right most of the time. I do better now that I know better, but I still get it wrong. But God's righteousness is completely different from man's righteousness. You can make mistake after mistake and still have God's righteousness. Read the story of David. As many mistakes as he made, God blessed him and honored him. Why? Because even though David was weak, consumed by lust, and faced challenges that drove him to despair, he loved God. When God corrected him, he repented. When God told him he was wrong, he did what he had to do to get right. No matter how far off into the deep end of sin David had gone, he never forgot who God was and sought His face anyway.

When you adopt this attitude of devotion toward God, He draws you close to Him because your sin does not keep you apart for long. No matter how bad the situation, how poor your choice was, He will place you high above evil. This position allows you to see the bigger picture. You're also far enough away from fear that it doesn't hinder your ability to hear God's voice. Then you start to see how powerful and mighty God really is.

Question for Reflection:

When was the last time I was in trouble and who did I turn to for help? Why?

Depression

He who dwells in the secret place of the Most High shall remain stable and fixed under the shadow of the Almighty [Whose power no foe can withstand]. -- Psalm 91: 1

Depression is often caused by physical or emotional imbalances, some of which may be the result of heredity. Depression also can stem from life situations that are overwhelming to us. It's easy to become unstable and fall apart in the face of adversity, to lose hope and become depressed — especially when you try to correct the situation in your own strength. You become exhausted, which only further feeds the depression.

I think the word "shadow" is used in this Scripture because it makes clear that you are behind or under God's protection. He acts like a shield to ward off all those sneak attacks that are waged against your mind. If you think about sitting beneath the shade of a tree while the scorching heat of summer is only footsteps away, you'll get an idea of what God's protection is like. It's not always the removal from deadly or harmful situations that you receive, but you always will be protected in the way that God designs to keep you safe for His greater purpose. But this can only work if you live in Him. When you live in Him you learn what He would have you do — despite how you feel. You also learn how to work through your sadness and anger instead of allowing these emotions to worsen and affect every area of your life. You will become stable while not allowing the instability of your circumstances to shake you.

Depression is not always short-term or easily improved. Sometimes you need assistance from trained professionals, and that relief is not inconsistent with also seeking the help of God. Whatever you do, just know that God wants you to be stable and whole . . . in His shadow and in His protection.

Consider this: If you are struggling with depression, don't be ashamed. There are many resources that can help you overcome it and deal with the root cause. When you have recovered, use the experience to help you grow closer to God.

You Can Be Safe in the Middle of Danger

You shall not be afraid of the terror of the night, nor of the arrow (the evil plots and slanders of the wicked) that flies by day, Nor of the pestilence that stalks in darkness, nor of the destruction and sudden death that surprise and lay waste at noonday. -- Psalm 91:4 – 5, AMP

God KNOWS. He knows that we face very real threats to our existence — disease, illness, hostility, war, unemployment, neighborhood violence. But yet He tells you not to be afraid of anything that can come against you. Why? He is almighty and all-powerful. His power works best in your weakness. His power is greater than anything you can face or experience. His forgiveness, His protection, and His power can be made real in your life. He knows the terrors you have faced and will face. He knows that sometimes you're caught offguard and that you didn't see it coming. He knows you will encounter situations that will create fear. He just doesn't want you to be shaken and paralyzed by this fear. Instead, He wants to stir up His power in you despite your fear. He knows your terrors are real, but He wants you to live beyond them. When you know His power is real and that it is greater than any threat that falls on you, your fears cannot consume you.

Questions for reflection:

What are the real threats I am facing right now?

How can God help me work through these problems despite my fear?

God's Protection and Preservation

For He will give His angels [especial] charge over you to accompany and defend and preserve you in all your ways [of obedience and service]. -- Psalm 91: 11, AMP

If you are obeying and serving God, He will order His angels to surround and protect you. This is good news when you are doing what He has called you to do. It's one thing to quit when you weren't supposed to be doing something. It's another matter altogether to quit when you are doing what God has called you to do, especially if this decision stems from fear about what others will do to you or think about you.

When God calls you to do something, He will protect you. When you understand the depth of this kind of protection, you come to understand that you have no reason to be afraid of anything or anyone. You also understand that God's power is greater than your fears, so fear does not have to paralyze you. Whatever you fear—whether it's losing friends, family support, or acceptance—just stop and think about all that God is promising you in this Scripture. His angels are defending you and preserving you from harm and danger. All you have to do is ask Him what He wants from you; then obey and serve. This is a great investment to make for all He's giving you in return. Yes, you may lose people or things that once seemed important. Yes, you may be terrified. But His angels will defend and preserve you as long as you keep obeying and serving.

Question for reflection:

Have there been times in my life where it was evident that God sent His angels to watch over me?

A Troubled Heart

So put away trouble from your heart, and put away pain from your body. Because the years when you were a child and the best years of your life are going by fast. -- Ecclesiastes 11: 10, NLV

I remember the words our command chaplain told us at a safety brief in January 2012. He said that whatever had us sad or angry at that moment, when we looked back on it a few years from now we would view it a lot differently. Therefore, there is nothing about our current suffering that is worth ending our lives over. Of course, he acknowledged that help in the form of mental health care might be necessary to get past those feelings. But his message was that ending your life or spending it in emotional and mental turmoil in response to difficult circumstances is not the answer.

I also would like to encourage you and tell you that whatever you're going through right now is not worth wasting the years of your youth. These days will be over before you know it. The moments of your youth are brief and God wants you to live them in joy, discovery, and fulfillment—not misery, depression, or suicidal ideation. He wants you to be able to look back on this time of your life and see goodness and growth and not just difficulty and struggling.

Questions for reflection:
Is there anything I'm struggling with at this time that seems like too much to handle on my own?

How can I get past it in a way that is pleasing to God?

Your Mental Soundtrack

All the days of the desponding and afflicted are made evil [by anxious thoughts and forebodings], but he who has a glad heart has a continual feast [regardless of circumstances]. -- Proverbs 15:15, AMP

Sometimes it's the things we tell ourselves about our circumstances that keep us anxious or depressed. It's easy to see why you would be consumed by certain troubling events, such as when a parent or close friend dies or when you've lost your job. But what you tell yourself in times like these is crucial. If you say, "I'll never recover" or "There's no way out," you have decided that your circumstances are catastrophic and impossible to overcome. If you tell yourself that, "Yes, this is difficult but I will get through it," your struggles will be temporary and you will overcome them. Take an inventory of what you tell yourself and what you think when you face difficult circumstances. If needed, change your mental soundtrack.

Questions for reflection:

What do I tell myself when I'm dealing with difficult circumstances?

What do I need to tell myself when I'm dealing with difficult circumstances?

Bitterness

Don't say, "I will get even for this wrong". Wait for the Lord to handle the matter. -- Proverbs 20: 22, NLT

Easier said than done, right? But I'm sure that if you take an honest look at your life, or listen to a true and trusted friend, you'll see that you pay the cost when you don't follow this Scripture. A desire for revenge is a telltale sign of bitterness.

It's completely understandable that when you are wronged, you want the person who wronged you to receive the consequences for their behavior. But when you meditate on how to pay someone back by any means necessary, you're harboring bitterness in your heart and eventually you could act out on what you've been planning. When we try to take revenge into our own hands, we might hurt the offender but we hurt ourselves as well. We're only feeding the bitterness. The person who hurt you may have taken something from you that you'll never get back. Or he may have physically harmed you. But the anger you feel and cling to is only hurting you. That person has gone on with his life, likely unaware of, and certainly unaffected by, your pain, while you move about your current existence as though this person is the reason you live, breathe, think and move.

God must be the reason for your existence and your choices. When you allow your desire for revenge to consume you, you are telling God that you don't trust Him to handle the matter. Even worse, you're saying that your plans to bring harm to another person are more important than the plans He has for you. Don't waste your youth on fantasies of revenge — especially when God has promised He will handle the matter in a perfect way that you never could.

Question for reflection:

The next time someone wrongs me, how can I trust God instead of giving into revenge?

Anger

Understand [this], my beloved brethren. Let every man be quick to hear [a ready listener], slow to speak, slow to take offense and to get angry. For man's anger does not promote the righteousness God [wishes and requires]. -- James 1:19 – 20, AMP

I don't interpret this Scripture to mean that you should never get angry. I do see it as God's way of warning you that what we often do with human anger is not pleasing to God. I've come to observe that our anger communicates a message far deeper than we probably intend. I suspect that man's anger is not pleasing to God because it's often focused on our own sense of our rights, equality, emotions and perceptions. We feel wronged in some way, slighted in what we think we deserve, and now want retribution.

Since we are unique individuals, the definition of wrong and right will vary depending on whose counsel you seek. Only God truly knows all the details from both sides of the story. Perhaps this is why He teaches us to listen more than speak and not to be easily angered. It also could be why human anger is usually not righteous. You could be perfectly justified in your anger because you saw or experienced something that just was not right. But your attempt to exact justice on your terms in reaction to the original offense is not God's righteousness.

I also believe God wants you to be slow to anger because a calm temperament is for your benefit. When you're quick to get angry, it shows people how to manipulate you. If they can control your emotions, they can control the way you think. Once this happens, you're out of God's order and will for your life. He gives you free will, but He doesn't want you to be manipulated by other limited beings or by Satan. He wants you to choose Him and to choose life. If you take the time now to discover why you're so angry and take this to God, He will honor you and help you work through it. He can replace your anger with the spirit of action to help others in a way that glorifies Him and replaces your angry heart with that of a servant.

Questions for reflection:

How have I reacted to things that make me angry?

In the future how can I deal with my anger in a godly way?

Don't Let Your Anger Meet Tomorrow

When angry, do not sin; do not ever let your wrath (your exasperation, your fury or indignation) last until the sun goes down.
-- Ephesians 4:26, AMP

Life is full of injustice—and I'm not talking about mere slights like being cut off in traffic. Innocent children are neglected and abused, people are raped and murdered, racism and sexism still exist, and sometimes the people who are supposed to support, love or guide us instead use or abuse us. It is understandable that you would be angry after witnessing or experiencing an injustice of this magnitude. The problem is when you stay angry, when it becomes the essence of who you are.

Anger in itself is not bad, but God does not want our anger to result in us committing sin. If you've prayed and asked God for deliverance and you still find yourself in a perpetual state of anger, it's time to seek help from a trusted friend, pastor or counselor. There may be a deeper issue that you need to resolve. Your youth is the perfect time to learn how to process and overcome anger. If you don't, you will spend more years than God ever intended in anger and frustration. Don't leave anger unchecked in your life. It opens the door to sin and God does not want that for you.

Questions for reflection:

Am I angry about something that I cannot let go of?

What can I do to get past it?

Courage Means Doing It Afraid

For if you keep silent at this time, relief and deliverance shall arise for the Jews from elsewhere, but you and your father's house will perish. And who knows but that you have come to the kingdom for such a time as this and for this very occasion? -- Esther 4:14

Esther was in a bad situation and if I had been her, I also would have been terrified to speak up.

She was a young Jewish woman who became queen to the Persian king. To make a long story short, the king listened to an evil advisor and decided that he was going to exterminate all the Jewish citizens of his kingdom, not realizing that Esther, his own wife, was Jewish. Esther found her courage and changed the course of events for all Jews. They were not exterminated because Esther found the courage to speak up and reveal the genocidal plan. Esther might have lived if she had remained silent, based on her position of royalty. But her cousin reminded her that God placed her in her position as queen and that it was not about her. His words probably reminded her that not only was she an unlikely candidate for the position of queen but that she had unlikely favor with the king. Therefore, God must have had a reason to put her where she was.

Sometimes as a young woman you need people to remind you that it's not all about you. It's easy to stand on the sidelines because you're afraid that getting involved in order to change a bad situation will harm you or cast you in a negative light. It's easy to believe that it's just not your problem. But if you act beyond your fear, God will bless you. If you don't, He'll use someone else and bless them. So let Him use you in your youth . . . you just might change the course for an entire generation.

Questions for reflection:

When has speaking up been difficult? Why?

How can I work through my hesitation to speak up in the future?

RELATIONSHIPS

In your walk with God, it is important that you establish a relationship with Him. In order to do this, you have to know Him and know His voice. I guarantee that once you know Him and see Him for who He really is, you will love Him. Once you love Him, you will love yourself. Once you love yourself, you can love others and relate to them in the way He meant for you.

Obedience is Better than Sacrifice

But Samuel replied, "What is more pleasing to the Lord; your burnt offerings and sacrifies or your obedience to his voice? Listen! Obedience is better than sacrifice, and submission is better than offering the fat or rams" -- 1 Samuel 15: 22, NLT

Did you know that one of the definitions for sacrifice is that it is a move in a game that is used to psych out the opponent? When I learned this, I understood the deeper message of the situation described in the above Scripture. To make a long story short, King Saul (King David's predecessor) did not do what Samuel told him to do. This basically constituted disobedience to God because Samuel was a man who was dedicated solely to God.

Saul had a history of disobedience, which started in his youth with insecurities he probably never resolved, and had such a lackluster relationship with God that God decided it was time for David to be anointed as the next king. I could not understand why God seemed so upset as to take away Saul's crown until I thought about sacrifice as playing a game with God. You give Him what you want to give up, as though He can't see you holding on to the very card you actually need to give up. Rather than just doing what He told you, and really repenting for what you did wrong, you decide that you will make things right your way. This means, in your heart, you have reduced God to an opponent in a game. This is not the relationship He wants with you. He wants your obedience because He knows what's best for you. He doesn't want your chosen sacrifice because that is only what *you* are willing to submit.

Questions for reflection:

Have I ever struggled to obey God? Why?

How can I develop an attitude of obedience towards God?

Favor from God

Many crave and seek the ruler's favor, but the wise man [waits] for justice from the Lord. -- Proverbs 29: 26, AMP

Our culture teaches us to seek favor from those with authority, power, celebrity and money. Now, there is nothing wrong with recognizing someone as an expert in a particular area and relying on his or her advice. There is also nothing wrong with establishing relationships with people who have strengths that you need — and who can assist you in developing your own strengths. And, you should definitely obey those who have authority over you. God wants you to form relationships with others for the building of His kingdom and simply for your enjoyment and benefit.

What God does not want is for you to seek approval from those with earthly authority. If you do, you'll find yourself going down a rough, winding path on which right and wrong become slanted to the values of those with whom you're talking. You are giving these people a position in your life that was only meant for God. True favor, justice and authority only come from God. He might use us to give favor to others, and He might give us favor with others, but it all really comes from Him. Young women who vow to change their focus from gaining the approval of others around them to learning how to please God have a whole lifetime in progressing toward success in life without worldly endorsements. This is not an easy feat. But start honing your focus now and it will become second-nature later your adulthood.

Questions for reflection:

How can I respect people in authority without seeking their favor?

How can I live to please God and still have godly relationships?

Real Service

Share your food with the hungry, and give shelter to the homeless.
Give clothes to those who need them, and do not hide from relatives
who need your help. -- Isaiah 58: 7, NLT

Your relationship to others — be it strangers, friends or family — should be one of service. Service is basically doing what *you* can to fill a practical need for someone else. If you know that what you have to offer won't fulfill the need, you can enlist help.

I said previously that God loves young go-getters. Well, He also loves young women who are willing to help and enlist help, those who have a heart to put others first. This doesn't mean that you allow others to take advantage of you because such people are not helping you grow in your relationship with God. It does mean that you should treat everyone the way you would want to be treated, and that you help them within your means and ability. You would want your family, friends or neighbors to help you if you had a practical need you couldn't fill or a serious problem that you needed help to resolve, wouldn't you? Whatever you do, don't hide from people who need you. God needs you to help others.

Questions for reflection:

Are there people in my life who need my help?

How can I help them in a way that will make a real difference to them?

Real Friends

Many will say they are loyal friends, but who can find one who is truly reliable? -- Proverbs 20:6

How do you distinguish real friends from acquaintances? Pay attention to what people do, not just what they say. It's very simple. A person will prove to be a friend by how reliable they are. She will keep your confidences, listen to you without ridiculing or judging, show up when expected, and support you in just the way you need. If someone is unreliable, she does need to be your friend, at least at this time.

If you aren't capable of offering this steadfast assurance in return, you aren't friend material right now, either. The good news is that you can always improve and encourage others to improve in this area of life. Until then, though, acknowledge how your unreliability can hurt someone else, and also be realistic about how someone else's unreliability can hurt you. Just keep God's will for your friendships first and remember that real, true friends are gifts from God. Allow Him to teach you how to be one and how to receive one.

Questions for reflection:

What else does the Bible say about real friendship?

What do I need to change to be a real friend and have real friends?

Parents

Whoever curses his father or his mother, his lamp shall be put out in complete darkness. -- Proverbs 20: 20, AMP

Many young women, even those who are blessed to have great parents, think that their mom and dad are wrong about almost everything. It's not until you've experienced life on your own that you realize there was truth to what they taught you, especially if they brought you up in a home that was rooted in the Word of God.

Until you reach this stage of understanding, just be careful not to do what this verse says. Treat your parents with respect and love, even when you disagree. This is not to dismiss any real issues you may have with your parents. This is also not meant to minimize any abuse you may have suffered at their hands. If you have experienced this, you need to take it to God in prayer and fasting, and ask for professional help to heal the past or to learn how to end a bad situation that still exists. Just remember that God is the one who truly knows good from evil and His guidance in your relationships with your parents is the most important tool you have.

Question for reflection:

Given my particular relationship with my parents, how can I honor them?

Gossip

A gossip goes around telling secrets, so don't hang around with chatterers. -- Proverbs 20: 19, NLT

I'm not sure why gossip is so popular in this current generation. Some of the entertainment that young women today love is based on spreading gossip. Just look at celebrity magazines and reality shows. Seeing such stories on the newsstands encourages us to gossip in our private lives.

There are two good ways to know if someone is a gossip. First, pay attention to what they tell you about other people. If they are always telling you private information about others, chances are they will repeat what you tell them to someone else. Second, if you tell them something you didn't tell anyone else and it gets back to you, you've been had by a gossip. The best way to deal with a gossip is to pray for them while also disassociating from them. This doesn't mean that you cut such people completely out of your life. It also doesn't mean that you can't talk to them. It does mean that you do not invite them to have a front row seat in your personal matters. You do not discuss your goals, dreams, fears, insecurities and past with them.

Sometimes it's hard to discern who is trustworthy with your confidence because we're wired to want intimacy with others, and intimacy is built by sharing personal time and information. But remember that pleasing God should be the ultimate goal of any relationship. You please God in your relationships by minding your business and being willing to disclose and draw out information only when it is intended in love and to help the other person. This isn't always easy to do and takes practice, but God will show you how if you pray and ask Him for guidance.

Questions for reflection:

Was there ever a time you disclosed sensitive and private information that someone told you in confidence? If so, what were your motives?

Has someone ever repeated something you told them in confidence? How did this affect you?

How You Live Your Life

Let everyone see that you are considerate in all you do. Remember, the Lord is coming soon. -- Philippians 4:5, NLT

Your behavior, habits and life speak louder to others than your words do, and God is near and coming soon to judge your actions. God cares about how you treat others because it reflects on Him and affects the outcome of salvation for the world.

God can speak directly to a person; it happens on several accounts in the Bible. But He also uses people to reach each other. He used others to help you, love you and assist you, and He wants to use you to do the same for them. Ultimately, though, He wants us all to play our parts in making salvation real for others. It starts with living a life that is desirable to those who do not believe in God or have strayed away from God. Being considerate is one of the easiest ways to do that. I know . . . no one wants to be taken advantage of. But when your focus is on glorifying God in everything you do and in every area of your life, God will take care of you so well that this will be a minor complication in God's ultimate plot and storyline.

Questions for reflection:

Are there any times in my life when being considerate and showing love to others has been difficult? Is so, why?

How can I remember how my treatment of others can contribute to their salvation?

God's Real Design for Marriage

But among the Lord's people, women are not independent of men, and men are not independent of women. For although the first woman came from man, every other man was born from a woman, and everything comes from God. -- 1 Corinthians 11:11-12, NLT

God's order never leads to oppression, racism, classism or sexism. With marriage in particular, many of us don't understand God's intention for it. Spousal roles become distorted into what they were never meant to be and the concepts of submission and order are viewed negatively, or as a justification to control or abuse another person. But in God's community, both those in authority and submission in a family or marriage have responsibility to each other. When God is the ultimate authority, no one in a marriage has to worry about being taken advantage of, being mistreated, or being misled. Likewise, the person in authority will answer to God for what goes on in the marriage and family. We all belong to God and when we consistently submit ourselves to His design and desire for authority and order, we can't lose.

Questions for reflection:

What are my current beliefs about the relationships of spouses and family members?

How do those beliefs differ from what God says about these relationships?

Making Excuses

Hot-tempered people must pay the penalty. If you rescue them once, you will have to do it again. -- Proverbs 19: 19, NLT

Trust me when I say that you never want to have a relationship in which you are the person who is always making excuses for the other's misconduct. If you do it once, you will do it again . . . and again and again. The person who expects you to cover for him has no personal sense of accountability or responsibility. Such people know that as long as they can push the blame onto another person, they don't have to answer for their actions; all they have to do is offer excuses and allow someone else to take the fall. If you associate with this type of person, you could suffer the consequences for behavior in which you never engaged. You don't want that. Life is hard enough without having to answer for someone who has no consideration for how their actions affect anyone else. Most importantly, you're assuming a role in their life that God never intended for you to assume. Only God should determine whether or not someone gets to pay the penalty. Pray and ask God to show you how to handle your interactions with people who have you assume their responsibilities. Pray for them, but love them from a distance.

Question for reflection:

Are there people in my life for whom I always make excuses?

Angry People

Don't befriend angry people or associate with hot-tempered people, or you will learn to be like them and endanger your soul. – Proverbs 22: 24 – 25, NLT

Association is a powerful thing. When you associate with a person, other people who don't know you well or at all will assume things about you based on this relationship. More personally, that person's moods, emotions, behavior and words will affect you. If they are always angry and speaking in negative terms, then guess what? You'll find yourself often angry and bring the same despondent attitude into the world.

The sad reality is that if you are normally a happy and positive person, you will not be the one providing the influence in this dynamic. Instead, the other person will wear you down and you more likely will adopt his negative attitude. You can, however, be a positive example from a distance. Everyone is not meant to have a front row seat in your life. Some people shouldn't even be in the building because they're so toxic. So be kind, an emotion that does not require you to be friends. Be careful not to share your personal thoughts and be mindful of the things they speak when they are in your presence. Above all, remember to guard your soul.

Questions for reflection:

Have I endangered my soul by associating with angry or toxic people?

How can I change this and associate with people who are uplifting and encouraging?

When God Doesn't Hear Your Prayers

God detests the prayers of a person who ignores the law. -- Proverbs 28: 8, NLT

It is easy to fall into the trap of thinking that certain rules apply to other people and not you. If you start to believe that only the rules you want to obey apply to you, you'll find ways to get around the rules that you don't want to follow. That's fine if you are content with a life in which you break rules or worse, commit illegal acts. But if your goal is to have a vibrant and ongoing relationship with God, this won't work.

This Scripture doesn't say that God ignores our prayers when we ignore rules; He *detests* them. This is not because God is punitive in nature and seeks to bless some and curse others. It's because it's in His nature to love good and hate evil. He created us in His image, so we are a part of Him. He hates to see us willfully do wrong. I believe He especially hates to see young women ignore the law and go their own way because you're at a time in your life where you should be laying the foundation for who God wants you to be, and not falling away from Him.

If you've fallen short or even shocked yourself with the things you've done, just go to Him and ask Him now to make it right. Because I also believe that He delights in the prayers of young women who know and obey His commands and strive to please Him regardless of the mistakes they've made.

Questions for reflection:

When have I ignored God's laws?

What consequences did I notice in my life during these times?

Associations

Young people who obey the law are wise; those with wild friends bring shame to their parents. -- Proverbs 28: 7, NLT

So not only do harmful associations negatively affect you, they have an impact on your family and real friends. We all have a propensity towards rebellion and disobedience. Your associations are one more way to establish your position in living a life for God or living a life in constant disobedience to God. Why? The people you enjoy being around have influence over you, which is why you spend time with them and invite them into your life. If they have influence over you, you'll likely find yourself adopting their philosophies about life, their behaviors and their attitudes. This can be why someone who starts off loving God and truly wanting to please Him can wind up living in sin and disobedience to God. Maybe their friends' lives presented an alternative that was attractive in some way, and so they decided to live the same way. And the person's godly friends and family members stand by in horror and shame, watching a loved one destroy her life. God is always watching you, and He wants you to be able to live a life that brings Him glory, as well as honor and joy to those He's placed in your life to love you.

Questions for reflection:

Do I have friends who rebel against God's laws?

Have I been the type of friend who encourages my friends to rebel against God's laws?

SEXUAL PURITY

Much of what is in this section was inspired by the fellowship discussions in the young adult ministry of which I was a part. Sexual purity is always a sore topic with young women. But guess what . . . it remains a difficult discussion as we grow older if we don't grow in our relationship with God.

God's intention is not to keep you from having sex; it's to keep you from having sex outside of His original design for this sacred act and from experiencing all the negative consequences that come with having sex outside of a covenant.

Do not be fooled by the world's message; sexual purity *is* possible in this world today. You just have to make the decision and know you are doing it for the right reasons. Once you do, God will honor and bless you in ways you never imagined.

The Marriage Bed

Marriage is honourable in all, and the bed undefiled: but whoremongers and adulterers God wiil judge." -- Hebrews 13:4, KJV

Only God gets to judge those who have sex outside of marriage. This isn't to say that you can just have sex outside of marriage with no consequences since God will forgive you. It does mean, however, that when you have premarital sex, God will not help you to become marriage material for a holy, godly union. An adulterer is not only someone who cheats on a spouse; an adulterer someone who is unfaithful to God.

I know . . . you're young. Maybe you feel like you're missing out because no one in this generation waits until marriage to have sex anymore. But God is faithful. When you're faithful to Him, He can make anything happen. Don't decide to abstain just because you want the reward God will give you. Do it because God is worthy of your faithfulness and your best. He won't waste your youth. He'll preserve you through it and then give you to the man or woman who will honor you like you've honored Him.

Questions for reflection:

If you have had sex: How can I become and stay celibate until marriage?

If you are a virgin: How can I maintain my virginity until marriage?

A Secluded Garden

A garden enclosed and barred is my sister, my [promised] bride — a spring shut up, a fountain sealed. -- Song of Solomon 4:12, AMP

I'm convinced that God desires sexual purity for us not just because it is holy but because it is for our protection. Think about all the messages and images the world gives and shows you about sex. For that matter, think about what your friends and family have told you about sex. Then think about what you've come to believe about sex. Chances are, unless you've been told and trained to believe the truth, you don't know or believe what God says about it.

God wants you to be like the enclosed garden. He doesn't want anyone leaving seeds in your soul that were never intended to be there, and He certainly doesn't want those seeds to bear the type of fruit He never intended for your soul to bear. He wants to be glorified even through your sexuality. This is opposite of what the world will tell you, and so you've probably made choices regarding your sexuality based on misinformation. But God can restore any person and any situation. He can help you understand your sexuality and restore you so you can become the secluded garden and purified fountain. If you have maintained your virginity, please know that God will honor you so don't buy into what the world says. If you have not, please know that you are not too far gone. Wherever you are, God can turn you around.

Questions for reflection:

What is my current belief about sexual purity?

What does God's Word say about sexual purity?

Soul Ties

Or do you not know and realize that when a man joins himself to a prostitute, he becomes one body with her? The two, it is written, shall become one flesh.-- 1 Corinthians 6: 16, AMP

Sex bonds you to another person. This Scripture uses the example of a man and a prostitute but the bonding occurs in any sexual union. If you don't believe this, think about how many times you wished you could stop having sex with the person you know is no good for you. You can justify it in a number of ways—you have needs, you're attracted to the person, you're "getting it out of your system" before the right person comes along—which will lead you to believe you can stop any time you want. Or maybe you were sexually abused or raped, and as a result you're struggling with your sexuality because of the damage that was done. You have an element or spirit grafted into your soul that was never meant to be there in the first place. These are called soul ties and only God can break them. If you invite God to have His way with this part of your life, you can be healed and made new. He can restore you and break those soul ties so that you're ready to be united with the man or woman He has for you.

Questions for reflection:

Do I have any soul ties?

How have they affected my life?

Breaking Soul Ties

But the person who is united to the Lord becomes one spirit with Him.-- 1 Corinthians 6:17, AMP

Within hours of asking God how soul ties are broken, I found this Scripture. I believe that the main factor in breaking soul ties lies in your ability to tie yourself to God. When you do this, you invite the Holy Spirit into your being. Once the Holy Spirit resides within you, you don't feel right doing the things you used to do and at some point you simply must stop. You're replacing painful or even good memories about another person with the beautiful Holy Spirit of God.

The Holy Spirit is powerful and amazing. Encounters with the Holy Spirit will leave you wanting more of the goodness that God has to offer and less of the earthly, fleshly experiences you've already had. You find yourself viewing your life through spiritual eyes. You no longer view your mistakes and your struggles as just bad or evil, and you learn to view them as a part of you—the part of you that God is making into a beautiful and awesome testament to His power and love. The process might look different for each person, but the end result is the same. Any previous soul ties no longer have any power over you, and you become a place where the Holy Spirit resides. You become connected to God.

Consider this: Pray and ask God to show you how you should break any soul ties of which He does not approve in your life.

Every Detail

The Lord directs the steps of the godly. He delights in every detail of their lives. -- Psalm 37: 23, NLT

God even delights in the details of our sexuality. If you are single that means God takes pleasure in teaching you to master sexual purity while He prepares you for the spouse He has for you. If you are married that means He takes pleasure in helping you learn how to have a sex life that pleases Him and satisfies you. This is possible when you learn His way for every area of your life. When you invite Him into every detail, He will show you what is good and what is not, what you are doing right and what you are doing wrong. When you invite Him into every detail, you don't need to hide from Him and you don't even try. When you invite Him into the details of your sexuality you open yourself to a new way of being and thinking.

When you learn the truth about living a godly life and honoring God in your sexuality, you won't want to live your life any other way. You may struggle getting there or even revert back to your old ways when you do get there. But don't give up. God is waiting to delight in every detail of your life . . . including your sexuality.

Questions for reflection:

What would God see if He saw my life right now?

What would make God delighted in my sexuality?

Sexual Sin

Run from sexual sin! No other sin so clearly affects the body as this one does. For sexual immorality is a sin against your own body. -- Romans 6:18, NLT

I used to wonder why sexual purity was such a big deal to God. After all, not everyone who engages in pre-marital sex is irresponsible. But through my interactions with others, group Bible study, and my own reading of the Bible, I've come to understand why sexual purity is important.

No other sin affects the body like sexual sin because it affects your body, mind, soul and spirit and has the same impact on the people with whom you engage in these acts. Sexual sin makes you susceptible to incurable STDs, unwanted and unplanned pregnancies, addictions, perversion and shame from committing sexual acts that you might not have wanted to do. I know this isn't news to you, but take a look at this from the perspective of trying to live a life that is pleasing to God. He doesn't want you to experience the hurt and harm that comes from sexual sin, and He doesn't want to lose you to a battle that you never had to fight. Yes, He can bring you out of anything, but He would much rather keep you safe and whole. If you are in sexual sin, it's not too late to come out of it. God is just a breath away. Decide today that you will honor God with your body and He will give you the strength to run from sexual sin.

Questions for reflection:

How has sexual sin negatively affected me?

What are the benefits of avoiding sexual sin?

Self-Control

A person without self-control is like a city with broken-down walls. --
Proverbs 25: 28

When you lack the self-control to abstain from any sexual activity that is not a part of God's original design for sex, you leave yourself open to a powerful spiritual attack. You might start out only engaging in certain acts and only with certain people. As time goes on, though, many find themselves doing things they never thought they would, sometimes with people with whom they never thought they'd even associate. Self-control becomes relative to their desires. But the truth about self-control is that you either have it, or you don't. The good news is that if you don't have this control, you can develop it.

The previous meditation's Scripture says that we are to run from sexual sin. Self-control will help you to avoid even being in situations that even look like they might be sexual sin. Then if you find yourself in such a moment, there's no question about what you should do . . . *run*! But in order to develop selfcontrol, you have to be honest about what the goal is and why you shouldn't keep falling into sexual sin. Then you have to resolve that you will do what it takes to avoid this sin. Ask God to give you wisdom, and hold on to His words whenever you are faced with a difficult temptation.

Questions for reflection:

How do I struggle with lack of self-control concerning sexual purity?

What steps do I need to take to make progress in these struggles?

The Kingdom of God

For be sure of this: that no person practicing sexual vice or impurity in thought or in life, or one who is covetous [who has lustful desire for the property of others and is greedy for gain] – for he [in effect] is an idolater – has any inheritance in the kingdom of Christ and of God. -- Ephesians 5:5, AMP

When I first read this, it was hard for me to understand why sexual sin in particular would cause anyone to forfeit their inheritance to the kingdom of God. But as I went deeper into the Word and learned more about what sexual sin is, I came away with a better understanding. I still need and want more insight, but I do know that sexual sin does not please God.

If you look at the state of the world today and consider how sex has played a part in it, you might see the severity of the problem, too. The legalization of pornography, adults who sexually abuse and rape children and get away with it, sexual trafficking of children and minors, prostitution, escort services, STDs with no cure, infidelity, children who are abused and neglected because they were unwanted – these are just some of the problems that stem from sexual sin. It always starts small, but it can spin out of control. You find yourself doing things that alter your sense of right and wrong. You hurt yourself and others in the process. And sometimes you don't recover. God does not want to withhold your inheritance from you. He wants you to be free from the acts and effects of sexual sin because He loves you and wants to bless you when you live right.

Question for reflection:

Why does sexual sin prevent my inheritance to God's kingdom?

Don't Be Fooled

Let no one delude and deceive you with empty excuses and groundless arguments [for these sins], for through these things the wrath of God comes upon the sons of rebellion and disobedience. --
Ephesians 5:6, AMP

I believe that God knows that sometimes you simply do not know any better than what you manage to do. He might allow you to experience the repercussions of your actions, but keep you from complete destruction so that you can learn from them. But He does want you to come to a place where you understand that sex outside of His original design is wrong and detrimental to your life. Once you know this and still continue to do what you were doing before, you open yourself to whatever the consequences may be for your actions.

Sometimes it's easy to disregard what you know God says is true when others (those close to you as well as those you don't know) make the argument for sexual sin an appealing one. But don't be fooled, God will repay them for their sins in His own way and time. He'll also repay you for yours if you follow their actions and disregard what you know He says is true.

Question for reflection:

How can I remember what God says is true about sex in light of the arguments others make?

ROMANCE

When I was in my late teens and early twenties, I had no idea the Bible gave a vivid, enticing account of what real romance looks like. I thought romance was supposed to be like the movies I saw or the books I read, most of which were not spiritually or biblically based. But after reading the Song of Songs, my limited view of romance was put to shame. And, this book made me view other accounts of romance and even totally unrelated Scriptures throughout the Bible differently. It also helped me realize that the only way I could experience this kind of love was by waiting for God to fulfill his promises in my life. I hope these Scriptures help you realize how deep romance can be and help you to wait for the husband or wife you truly want.

The Boaz Type

And now, my daughter, fear not. I will do for you all you require, for all my people in the city know that you are a woman of strength (worth, bravery, capability). -- Ruth 3:11

Boaz was a man who was slow to respond to love and romance, but willing to provide love as well as cherish and protect the one he loved. I think he may have had some insecurities that probably made him believe a woman like Ruth would never truly love a man like him. Ruth was an outsider in his community and I'm sure there were other women from his same cultural background that would have gladly married him. But he was a man who knew a good woman when he saw one and eventually rose to the occasion of doing what was right. He also saw more than what was on the outside. He appreciated all of the amazing qualities Ruth had to offer, and intended to honor her because of them.

My sisters in Christ, it's not always the handsome smooth operator who deserves your heart. Sometimes you have to be willing to give the regular guy a chance to win you over. If you ever meet him, pray that God makes the connection plain for you — if that's what He wants for you. If you don't, you could be missing out on the romance of a lifetime.

Questions for reflection:

What do I believe about romance?

What does God's Word say about romance?

Tall, Dark and Handsome

...He was dark and handsome, with beautiful eyes. And the Lord said, "This is the one"... -- 1 Samuel 16: 12

I'm going to take this Scripture out of its usual context. My sisters in Christ . . . can you imagine meeting some tall, dark, handsome man with beautiful eyes? You lock eyes for a minute, but then you look away thinking he's just another flirt. But there's something about him, and he must think the same thing about you because now he's crossing the room to talk to you. Days, weeks, months later you still aren't sure about his motivations. But there's something about him. There's something about him that lets you know he's trustworthy, that he deserves your heart. That "something" is God. When you have a real, right relationship with God, He can make a real love connection plain as day to you. You won't have to be reckless with your heart, hoping and wondering if this one is the one. All you have to do is listen and then enjoy the experience!

Question for reflection:

How can I let God lead my next potential connection?

When You Stand Out To Him

Solomon replied, Like the lily among thorns, so are you, my love, among the daughters. -- Song of Solomon 2: 2, AMP

Men know when they've met someone who is not like any other woman they've known. It seems like it happens immediately—almost in the blink of an eye. This means that once a young woman is ready to be found and her husband finds her, he will recognize that she is the one for him.

Notice the stark contrast that Solomon uses to describe the woman with whom he's in love and the other women he's known up until he met her. There's a lot to be said for this comparison. But what you must understand is that what is for you, is for you alone. In God's economy, there is no such thing as a man shortage. It just depends on whether or not you need preparation or the right moment and opportunity to meet the one God has for you. God knows the hearts of all people. So ask Him to help you be the best young woman that God has created you to be. Then get ready to be recognized as the one who stands out and enjoy the journey of romance—the way God designed it.

Questions for reflection:

What makes a young woman stand out to me?

What characteristics should I be looking for?

When He Stands Out

Like the finest apple tree in the orchard is my lover among other young men. I sit in his delightful shade and taste his delicious fruit. -- Song of Solomon 2: 3, NLT

My young sisters in Christ, you know when a young man is different. He doesn't treat you like a prize to be won. He shows you how much he likes and loves you. He mirrors God's idea of love and romance, not the world's. Spending time with him is like getting an idea of what having a godly covering over your life is like. It's refreshing and a new experience. It's just one of many ways that you know God loves you; He took the time to send you someone who sees you like He does. Never forget this. The man God has for you will stand out from the rest. When you submit completely and wholeheartedly to God, there will be no question in your mind about who he is.

Questions for reflection:

What makes a young man stand out to me?

What characteristics should I look for?

Love at the Right Time

Promise me, O women of Jerusalem, by the gazelles and wild deer, not to awaken love until the time is right. -- Song of Songs 2:7, NLT

God wants the best for you when it comes to romantic love, my young sisters. The best for you is who He has designed especially for you. Each of us will meet people who are a great fit for us. And as long as you're out in the world living your purpose and doing what brings glory to God, you don't have to worry about these encounters happening.

Young men will come along who appear to be the real thing. They look good to you, you look good to them, and it seems like God would approve of them. Just be careful not to awaken love before its time. God can help you discern what seems real from His best. If you ask Him to rule over your romantic life, He will show you His best for you. Until then, just enjoy dating and making friends. If you honor God, He'll bring you to the one to whom He wants you to give your heart.

Questions for reflection:

Am I romantically involved with anyone who seems like God's best? If so, what has God told me about this person?

How can I make different choices in the future when I date someone who seems like they could be God's best?

No Flaws

[He exclaimed] O my love, how beautiful you are! There is no flaw in you! -- Song of Solomon 4:7

Your brothers in Christ are visual and therefore moved by what they see. That's wonderful because it means that they can see beyond what a person says and pay attention to what they do and how they present themselves. This can, however, become a problem when their assessment of you is based primarily or solely on your physical beauty, and they decide that you look good enough to be their wife. Now, I'm not saying they should "settle" and marry a woman who is unattractive to them. I am saying that there is more to you than your physical appearance — and they'll never know if they can't get past what you present on the outside.

Your brothers in Christ are wired to win a woman's heart and treasure it. This is where true romance lies, and it's not always the most physically beautiful woman who will be able to give them the experience of pursuing a woman and working to maintain her love. So allow a man to take in your physical appearance, but don't forget to allow him to see the beauty of your soul and the potential for real romance. If you can accept your flaws, and he can as well, you just might experience the romance and love of a lifetime.

Question for reflection:

How can I focus on a my inner qualities and not just my outward appearance?

More than Words

His voice and speech are exceedingly sweet; yes, he is altogether lovely [the whole of him delights and is precious]. -- Song of Solomon 5: 16

There are two main points I want to draw out for my sisters in Christ. First, don't be totally moved by what he tells you. I think as women, we tend to get so emotionally attached to and moved by what we hear. Of course you want someone who will compliment you, tell you he loves you and say things to build you up and not tear you down. But if his actions and behavior don't match his words, he's not someone to whom you want to give your heart. Not only that, but it's only a matter of time before his words match the negative, destructive or abusive behavior you are already seeing. Second, if his words and actions line up, wait for God to show you whether or not he is right for you. No man (as in person) is perfect or has it all together. But, if you invite the Holy Spirit into your friendship and dating process, He can show you the red flags you might not want to see because you're so moved and stirred up emotionally by what the man in front of you is saying.

My young sisters, being in love is a wonderful experience. Just make sure that you allow God to guide it.

Question for reflection:

How can I focus on a young man's inner qualities and not just what he tells me?

MARRIAGE

As I write this I am single. So, I'm not offering you anything based on the personal experience of a successful marriage. But the Word of God is never wrong. In fact, it's helped me see ways that young women can get ready for marriage or improve their marriages if they already are married. Now that you've gotten this far, you can see how the Word of God can change you, your relationships and other areas of your life. If you are still single, let these lessons prepare you for marriage and help you be the spouse God is calling you to be. If you are married with children, I pray that they encourage you.

God as Husband

And it shall be in that day, says the Lord, that you will call Me Ishi [my Husband], and you shall no more call Me Baali [my Baal]. --
Hosea 2:16, AMP

When you view God as the ultimate bridegroom, your view of marriage has to change. If you think of the traditional roles of a husband and wife, the husband is typically the one who manifests his love in the roles of provider and protector. However, when you view God in these capacities and put Him first in your life, your perspective of your husband will be different. You'll come to understand that he was never meant to fulfill every need in your life – only the ones for which God created them. God takes care of the rest.

If you go into or through your marriage believing that your spouse is unfit for you because he cannot meet every need you have, it's possible that you need to change your perspective of who God is. This doesn't mean that you shouldn't ask for what you need. But you will never be happy in your marriage expecting your spouse to do what only God can do. God wants His rightful place in your life; he wants to be obeyed, respected, loved and trusted. He wants to be the ultimate husband and provide what only He can provide— total fulfillment. Just imagine what a marriage between two totally fulfilled young people would be like. Stick with God and you can find out.

Questions for reflection:

Does my view of God have to change to see Him as my husband?

How does this change my views and beliefs of the roles of husbands and wives in a marriage?

A Good Thing

He who finds a wife finds a good thing and obtains favor from the LORD. -- Proverbs 18:22, ESV

That's right, my young sisters in Christ. A MAN finds a wife! This means that your husband will find you. And not only does he find you, he receives the favor of God when he does.

I know this generation is filled with opportunities for speed dating, online dating, and other types of social activities for singles. While anything is possible with God, don't use these to make things happen in your own time. Let God guide you and allow things to happen on God's timeline. Make yourself findable, but hide your heart in God like a treasure box for which a worthy partner must really search. The right man will never stop until he finds you because he realizes the riches that await him.

Now, I'm not saying to make it difficult for the right man to get to know you. I'm just saying I want you to realize that your heart and your love are a treasure. God wants to hide your treasure so that it will only be received by the man He knows will cherish you. So the next time you think about finding a husband, remember that God already has that worked out. Pray and ask God to "hide you in plain sight." Then make yourself findable and be ready.

Question for reflection:

How can I make myself findable?

God's Desire for Raising Children

Drink waters out of your own cistern [of a pure marriage relationship], and fresh running waters out of your own well. Should your offspring be dispersed abroad as water brooks in the streets? [Confine yourself to your own wife] let your children be for you alone, and not the children of strangers with you. -- Proverbs 5:15 – 17, AMP

I believe one of God's purposes for marriage is to create and raise children in a stable environment with love, discipline and a living example of God's Word. If you don't agree, that's okay. But I challenge you to talk to anyone who grew up not knowing either or both of their biological parents. As children, they did not have access to basic information about themselves because they did not know who or what they came from. When the questions they have about themselves remain unanswered into adulthood, they struggle with trying to figure out who they really are. Even worse, they struggle with the implications and trauma of illegitimacy, abandonment and abuse from broken family bonds. They spend valuable, irreplaceable time trying to overcome what never should have been.

When family is created in God's design of marriage, problems will come up, but with God at the center, they can be managed without damaging the children involved. In God's world order, children have a birthright to be born into families where they are wanted, loved and raised to know God. If you don't know how to honor this responsibility, just ask God to show you how and He will use you to bless the next generation.

Question for reflection:

How can I change to become the spouse and parent God has called me to be?

The Spouse of Your Youth

And did not God make [you and your wife] one [flesh]? Did not One make you and preserve your spirit alive? And why [did God make you two] one? Because He sought a godly offspring [from your union]. Therefore take heed to yourselves, and let no one deal treacherously and be faithless to the wife of his youth. -- Malachi 2:15, AMP

God honors marriage and takes it seriously. When young people come together in a marital union, He wants to bless your union to create godly children. This isn't exactly the belief system by which young adults today live, and I understand why. A lot of the messages you get are the same ones I got growing up and then well into my young adulthood. You're taught to chase after careers, financial stability, professional achievements and admirable statuses. Then, you find someone who's at "your level," which is why we tend to marry so late in life, if we marry at all. And America as a whole doesn't have the same attitude towards family as people did in biblical days. This isn't necessarily a bad thing; it's just that we are a different generation living in a different world than our ancestors. But not all hope is lost. You can believe that God values marriage and family and then learn how to value these things yourself. Become a woman who leaves a mark on the world with godly children. Seek His will in this area of your life and ask for His guidance.

Questions for reflection:

Is my marriage one in which godly children can grow and flourish?

If not, how can my spouse and I work on making our marriage a godly marriage?

Getting Along

It is better to dwell in a corner of the housetop [on the flat oriental roof, exposed to all kinds of weather] than in a house shared with a nagging, quarrelsome, and faultfinding woman. -- Proverbs 21:9, AMP

I laughed when I first read this verse a few years ago. The NLT says it would be better to live in the corner of an attic than in the house with an argumentative woman. The corner of an attic! When I looked beneath the surface meaning I realized why men might feel this way. Men may be the head of the household, but women set the tone. When the woman is unhappy, it's highly likely that everyone else is as well.

My young sisters in Christ, as wives and mothers you have tremendous power. By your presence, behaviors and examples, you determine whether or not your family members feel good about themselves and the contributions they make in your household and in the community. If you are unmarried and have no children, you can use this time now to learn how to find the good in others and to treat them with dignity and kindness. God created you to nurture the right spirit—His spirit—in others. Embrace your power and the awesome ability He's given you, and nurture it for His glory.

Questions for reflection:
How can I make my husband and children feel loved and feel good about who they are?

How can I make others feel good about who they are?

FAMILY LIFE AND RAISING CHILDREN

Children are amazing. Some of the things they say are so simple yet so profound. If you spend enough time around them, you'll understand why they are a blessing to any family. If you have children, you know that they are a tremendous responsibility. They are also an awesome opportunity. As a young parent, you get to grow into your full adulthood while raising your children to be the next generation of godly adults. As you grow and change, they grow and change. As you allow God to mold you into the woman He has created you to be, you become better at molding your children to become the people God created them to be. If you are still single, use these lessons to prepare you for motherhood if that's a desire of your heart.

Bless Your Children

An inheritance obtained too early in life is not a blessing in the end. -- Proverbs 20:21, NLT

You usually don't appreciate anything that's free, items for which you didn't have to work pay. That's why overindulging children with material possessions without teaching them the importance of appreciation and hard work usually has disastrous results. Qualities such as selfishness, impatience, and entitlement often surface later on in life when these kids become adults. They believe that they are entitled to the best that life has to offer without waiting or working for it.

I can only imagine how painful it must be to watch the child you love become an adult who has no respect for how hard someone else had to work for what they have. As a parent, I would think that you want to bless your children and not curse them. But you set them up for failure when you give them everything without requiring them to respect and appreciate what it takes to get those things. You turn your blessings into curses. It is best to train your children while they are young, but it is never too late to do your part in getting them back on the right track. This won't guarantee a successful change in their behaviors or attitudes, but at least you will have done what God has called you to do as a parent — to bless your children and not curse them.

Question for reflection:
How can I teach my children to appreciate material possessions?

Train Your Children the Right Way

Train up a child in the way he should go [and in keeping with his individual gift or bent], and when he is old he will not depart from it. [Eph. 6:4; II Tim. 3:15.] -- Proverbs 22: 6, AMP

I love the AMP version of this Scripture because it provides two very valuable guidelines for raising children. First, there are things that never change when raising children in a godly home, such as respect for parents and those in authority, treating others right, obeying laws, and loving God. All of these things and more are found in the Bible. Once you as a parent learn the ways in which God wants you to live, you can teach those things to your children.

Second, every child is unique, with his own personality, talents and gifts. You wouldn't necessarily treat a child who is an extroverted budding scientist the same way you would a child who is a sensitive, introverted artist. You would seek to understand what that child needs from you in order to grow into a capable adult in this world. Remember the goal is to train a child in the ways of God and in a way that nurtures his or her disposition and gifts. Your children will remember what you do or do not do. Give them the blueprint that will help them be successful wherever they go in life.

Questions for reflection:

What personality and character traits do my children have?

How can I raise them with godly standards in light of these traits?

Don't Spare the Rod

He who spares his rod [of discipline] hates his son, but he who loves him disciplines diligently and punishes him early. -- Proverbs 13: 24, AMP

Hate is a strong word. But it helps you understand what you do to your children when you do not discipline them. The rod of discipline is the part of parental love that does not allow a child to destroy themselves or others. It does not allow a child to develop unhealthy habits and attitudes, treat others poorly, or deviate from godly rules and standards. All of these things — habits, attitudes, interaction with others, and living out God's commands — work together to affect the type of life a child will have as she grows into an adult. To abdicate the responsibility you have as a parent to shape your children in key areas is ultimately setting them up for failure.

The Amplified version of the Bible also helps you to see that correction, discipline and punishment are most effective early in a child's life. Something else I believe based on this Scripture is that if are young, you have an awesome opportunity to grow into adulthood as you shape your children for the same future. When you actively participate in their formation based on godly discipline and love, it helps shape you into the man or woman God wants you to be.

God smiles when His way is honored. Not everyone gets to experience this role of pleasing God through parenting, so treasure it and enjoy it. Above all, take the job seriously and you will enjoy the fruits of your labor.

Questions for reflection:

What am I already doing right to help my child live a godly life?

What more can I do to discipline my child in a way that honors God?

Bless Your Children by Your Example

The godly walk with integrity; blessed are their children who follow them. -- Proverbs 20: 7, NLT

One of the easiest ways to teach your children godly values and behaviors is to live them out yourself. If you watch your children or hear reports from others regarding the things they say and do, then find yourself wondering, "Where did they learn that?" maybe it's time to think about the example you set every day.

Children want your love, attention, guidance and discipline. Give them what they need and God will bless you. Now, the other part to this is that your children have free will just like you do. They don't have to follow your example. But if they choose to walk with you, be prepared by living an example that will bless them and not lead them further away from God.

Question for reflection:

What type of example am I setting for my children?

The Heart of a Child

A youngster's heart is filled with foolishness, but physical discipline will drive it far away. -- Proverbs 22:15, NLT

Just let me say that I do not promote spanking children. I could go deeper into my personal beliefs about it, but I won't. I will say, though, that you have to be mindful of the intent behind this type of discipline you choose and the spirit in which you do it. There are laws that can turn physical discipline into child abuse. Yet, the Word of God is safe and true and tells us that physical discipline corrects the innate foolishness that is bound up in the heart of children. Note that the version I selected describes physical discipline — not specifically beating, spanking, hitting, or yelling. The motive behind anything that God commands you to do is love. So ask yourself before you physically discipline your child if what you are planning to do will ultimately show His love. Love disciplines and corrects because it sees the harm ahead if corrections are not made. Ask God if what you are about to do is pleasing to Him and will result in raising your children into the person He has created them to be.

Questions for reflection:

What are my current beliefs about physical punishment and discipline for children?

What else does God's Word say about this?

How You Treat your Children Matters to God

Fathers, do not provoke your children to anger by the way you treat them. Rather, bring them up with the discipline and instruction that comes from the Lord. -- Ephesians 6:4, NLT

I believe that God has a special place in his heart for children and teenagers. They're dependent on parents and caregivers and what they experience and maybe suffer at the hands of these adults often affects who they are throughout their lives. I think this is why the Bible says that anyone who causes a child to sin is better off tying a weight to his neck and drowning himself in the sea.

Being too busy for your children, speaking harshly to your children, abusing them or failing to do any more than provide for them financially — these are just a few examples of behaviors that grieve the heart of God. God wants you always to show your children His ways. He knows you're not perfect and that you'll make mistakes in raising them. But He'll gladly help you overcome those mistakes according to His will if you strive to treat your children with His love.

Question for reflection:

Do I always aim to treat my children in a way that would please God?

How to Build a Life

Through skillful and godly Wisdom is a house (a life, a home, a family) built, and by understanding it is established [on a sound and good foundation], and by knowledge shall its chambers [of every area] be filled with all precious and pleasant riches. -- Proverbs 24:3 – 4, AMP

A life, home and a family are solidly built through godly knowledge, wisdom and understanding. God never equips you to know everything. He does equip you to gain knowledge and understanding of Him and His ways, and apply the wisdom you acquire to your life.

As you apply God's word in the areas of family and marriage, you'll see the results God intended specifically for your life. This isn't to say that you'll never make mistakes or that things will turn out the way you want when you did everything you were supposed to do. But godly wisdom is a tree of life that can transform any person and any situation in the direction of God's will. When you build your life on this wisdom, possibilities are endless.

God wants your life to flourish for generations to come. You're never too young to start building the kind of life God wants you to have. Ask Him for His knowledge, understanding and wisdom and you'll never go wrong.

Questions for reflection:

What's the difference between godly knowledge, understanding and wisdom?

How can I attain all three and apply them to my life?

If you enjoyed this devotional, please visit http://www.authorofmyfaith.com.

To contact Afi, e-mail: afi@authoroffaithmin.com.

REFERENCES

Amplified Bible copyright (c) 1954, 1958, 1962, 1964, 1965, 1987. La Habra, CA: The Lockman Foundation.

Amplified Bible (2010). Kindle Edition: Zondervan.

Bible Gateway (2012). Various Bible verses retrieved from http://www.biblegateway.com/.

NLT Study Bible. NLT Study Bible is an edition of the Holy Bible, New Living Translation. Holy Bible, New Living Translation, copyright © 1996, 2004, 2007. Carol Stream, IL: Tyndale House Foundation.

NLT Study Bible (2008). Kindle Edition: Tyndale House Publishers.

The Truth Project (2012). Developed by Focus on the Family. Study information retrieved from http://www.thetruthproject.org/.

www.ingramcontent.com/pod-product-compliance
Lightning Source LLC
Chambersburg PA
CBHW031623040426
42452CB00007B/650